Up and Running

UP AND RUNNING

Integrating Information Technology
and the Organization

Richard E. Walton

HARVARD BUSINESS SCHOOL PRESS
Boston, Massachusetts

93 92   5 4 3

Library of Congress Cataloging-in-Publication Data

Walton, Richard E.
   Up and running: integrating information technology and the
organization/Richard E. Walton.
      p.   cm.
   Includes index.
   ISBN 0-87584-218-6
   1. Management information systems.   2. Information technology.
I. Title.
T58.6.W345   1989
658.4038—dc20   89-35745
                                                                 CIP

CONTENTS

PREFACE

Information technology systems usually fall short of their potential—and the fault invariably lies in the failure to understand and manage the mutual influences of technology and organization throughout the extended implementation process. By "extended implementation process" I refer to a stream of activities and conditions, from some that occur even before a particular technology system is developed to others that modify the system after it has been put into practice. This book presents concepts, propositions, and action guidelines for better implementation.

My interest in writing this book has grown over the past decade as I studied how information technology (IT) and organization interact. My studies have covered office automation and decision-support systems, advanced manufacturing technologies, and shipboard technologies; they have treated the social consequences of IT and the human resource policies required to implement it; and they have analyzed the implementation process itself and the organizational and labor relations contexts that lead to effective systems. Cumulatively, this work convinces me that advanced information technology is becoming the single most powerful force shaping the structure and functioning of modern work organizations and, conversely, that managing the organization well is absolutely key to exploiting the potential of this extraordinary technology. Whether one's primary interest is in the technology or organizational behavior, one must come to terms with the other.

I have written this book for two broad audiences: practitioners and scholars. The practitioner audience includes leaders who formulate IT policies and set the direction for organizational development and change, and others who plan and execute IT systems.

The scholarly audience includes researchers whose primary interest is in information systems and academics in the field of organizational behavior. Both groups have a stake in better knowledge and technique to promote the mutual adaptation of IT and organizations.

The driving force behind this book is the same for both audiences—to influence practice, in one case directly, in the other indirectly, and to improve how we put this powerful and versatile resource to work for society. The first step is to close the gap between rhetoric and practice.

Planners acknowledge more about the interdependence of IT and organizations than they act upon. They may appreciate that technology will have organizational side effects, but they make little or no effort to predict or manage them. Suspecting that human consequences often undermine the technical and economic effectiveness of systems, planners nonetheless seldom systematically assess and diagnose these effects. While they often acknowledge that the interactions between information technologies and organizations can be dynamic and reciprocal, revealing themselves over time, planners have only belatedly begun to treat system development as an evolutionary process that may never be completed.

These discrepancies persist because planners' general appreciation of the relationship between IT and organization is seldom accompanied by an understanding of the "hows," "whys," and "so whats" of their interdependence. A second reason they persist is a lack of knowledge about how to coordinate the design and introduction of information technology with the design and introduction of organizational change.

I hope this book will help to fill both voids. It illustrates, in concrete terms, the variety of ways in which information technology and organizational dynamics can impinge upon one another, both positively and negatively, *depending on implementation choices*. Of equal importance, the book provides new ways to think about managing the organizational aspects of the implementation process, and identifies techniques to help manage it.

Focused as it is on the relationship of organization and information technology, this book complements other books on implementing IT, covering such topics as management of the corporate information services function, make-or-buy decisions, and techniques for identifying the strategic business contributions of IT. The books of McFarlan and McKenney, Gerstein, Gibson and Jackson, Keen, and Long come to mind. It also complements books that treat specific aspects of IT and organization in greater depth, for example, Zuboff's exploration of the consequences of workplace IT for power relations and the meaning of work, and Pava's sociotechnical analysis of office technology.[1]

ACKNOWLEDGMENTS

In writing this book, I am indebted to the Harvard Business School Division of Research, which supported the project, and to those with whom I have collaborated in studying information technology: Wendy Vittori, with whom I studied office technology; Leslie Schneider, my associate in the study of union-management relations and new technology; Gerald Susman, with whom I collaborated in a National Research Council study of advanced manufacturing technology installations in American industry; Shoshana Zuboff and Gloria Schuck, with whom I am investigating instructive examples of information technology; and Robert McKersie, my partner in contributing to the synthesis of work in the MIT project "Management in the Nineties." Susman, Zuboff, and McKersie also commented helpfully on this manuscript.

I am grateful to other colleagues who read and commented on the manuscript—Lynda Applegate, Chris Argyris, Michael Burns, James Cash, Warren McFarlan, James McKenney, Stanley Mihelick, and Kathleen Scharf. I also want to acknowledge the authors of the several published case histories I have drawn upon for this book, including John Carroll and Constance Perin, James Cash and Keri Ostrofsky, James Dean, Joel Fadem, Sabra Goldstein and Janice Klein, Dorothy Leonard-Barton, Beth Lewis, Enid Mumford, Brian Pentland, Thomas Richman, Gloria Schuck and Shoshana Zuboff, and Robert Thomas. With few exceptions, they read how I planned to use their material, made helpful suggestions, and provided additional information that I used to strengthen my analysis.

Finally, I want to thank Laurie Title for her good humor, patience, and expert assistance in managing the manuscript from start to finish.

INTRODUCTION AND OVERVIEW

This book is about effective implementation of advanced information technology (IT) in organizations. A major premise is that this task is a function of integrating the technical aspects of IT systems and the social aspects of organizations. This involves mutual and ongoing adaptation. For the executives who shape the IT strategies, the specialists who design IT systems, and the managers who introduce them, I prescribe and discuss the implications of practices that will encourage and sustain such adaptation.

The book is based on field research—my own and that of others. It relies heavily on documented case histories of the implementation of manufacturing and office technologies drawn from 19 separate entities—17 companies, 1 hospital, and 1 government agency. I report on both positive and negative examples to demonstrate good practice with IT systems used by workers, professionals, and managers for materials resource planning, computer-integrated manufacturing (CIM), database management, decision support, expert analysis, and end-user computing.

Relatively early in the history of computer technology, researchers prescribed the importance of the following propositions for IT implementation: project champions; top management support; good relationships between developers and user departments; user involvement; adequate organizational resources; communication; and a supportive organizational climate, for example, one that promotes an attitude of trust.[1]

These conditions continue to be important in today's IT environment. But as managers and researchers continue to learn how to implement IT effectively, new facets of some of these factors have come to light. "Top management support," for example, has expanded into a more ambitious concept—that top management should do more than merely support projects it approves. It should develop and promulgate a broad vision of IT, a vision capable of inspiring and guiding specific IT projects. Similarly, "user involvement," which in an earlier era referred to techniques for asking users for information that developers could use, is increasingly being replaced by a concept of broad participation by stakeholders, that is, all parties who will be affected by IT. Additionally, users are increasingly viewed as legitimately influencing design as well as installation activities.

In part, these and other evolutions in the requirements for effective implementation result from changes in IT itself, including the tendency for it to be used more strategically and to affect more elements of the organization in more ways; in part, they grow out of experience.[2]

A unique characteristic of advanced IT is its "dual potentialities" (or multiple potentialities)—the ability of a technology to produce one set of organizational effects or their opposites. For example, IT can either routinize work or it can widen the discretion of users; it can strengthen hierarchical control or facilitate self-management and learning by users. In short, managers can use IT to reinforce a strategy that relies upon employee compliance, or they can use it to promote an organizational context that elicits employee commitment. A company's organizational philosophy may prescribe which of these effects is preferred. But even when top management clarifies the intended effects of a system and guides the design, the managers and users who operate it can, and often do, interpret the system differently.

The dual potentialities of IT significantly raise the stakes for careful implementation. They define one of the major challenges with which the implementation process must deal if it is to be effective.

THE PROPOSED FRAMEWORK

Underlying the book's prescription for and illustration of practice is a rudimentary theory, the basic framework of which is suggested in Figure I-1. (A more detailed summary is provided in Figure 10-1 in the concluding chapter.) The essence of the theory is that an extended implementation process comprises three phases. In the first phase, management shapes the context before development of a specific IT system is begun; in the second, the design of the IT system takes place; and in the third, the system is introduced, operated, and diffused.

The term "implementation" is given a variety of meanings in the literature. Sometimes implementation is limited to activities that introduce systems but exclude the design process. In other writ-

Figure I-1.   IT Implementation Activities, Key Ingredients of Effectiveness, and Results

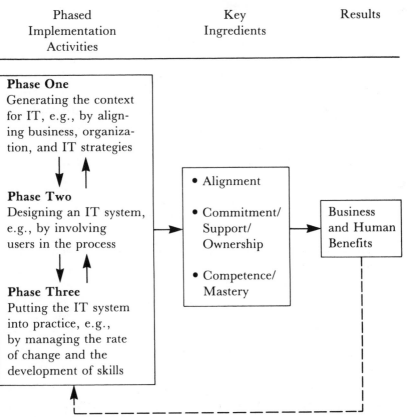

ings, implementation refers to both the design and introduction activities, but not to the activities that take place even earlier to create the contextual conditions for a successful employment of IT. In this book, the idea of an extended implementation process embraces all of these activities. I prefer this broad formulation of the subject because it is necessary to manage all of these phases of the process effectively. Moreover, the phases—of creating a favorable context, designing the system, and putting the system into practice—are interrelated and overlapping.

Earlier forms of information technology followed a relatively straightforward and common pattern of development. Design was succeeded by introduction, assessment, and, in some cases, diffusion. As systems have taken more varied forms and tackled unstructured as well as highly structured tasks, the pattern of development has become increasingly variable. One technology-consulting firm advocates maintaining a portfolio of methodologies for information system development. The choice for a given system would reflect the amount of change in business functioning and the degree of technological challenge involved.[3] The greater the business change and technical challenge, the more evolutionary the development methodology, revolving around cycles of "build it, try it, change it."

Economic or other commercial results are usually the most direct index of how well an implemented system is realizing its potential. My criteria also include the human effects. The relevant results of effective implementation are thus twofold.

- The economic purposes of the enterprise should be well served by the IT system, for example, by improvements in productivity, innovation, service, delivery, and so forth.
- The system's effects on the organization's members should be positive, for example, enhanced satisfaction and development.

The ability of management to produce these results depends upon whether its actions promote certain conditions which I propose are essential for effective implementation. In their general form, these key ingredients are (1) *alignment* of business, organizational, and technological strategies, (2) *commitment* of employees to, and support of stakeholders for, an IT system, and (3) *competence* of employees.

These conditions become increasingly specific as implementation progresses (see Figure I-2). Ultimately, in the introduction and operation phase, they take the form of:

- *Operational alignment:* The system in practice is consistent with the company's technology, organization, and business strategies, which are themselves aligned.
- *User ownership:* The system in practice is owned by strongly committed users.
- *User mastery:* The system in practice (and the task purpose it serves) is mastered by its users, who continue to learn and who, ideally, influence the system's further evolution.

Deficiencies in any of these areas can be harmful. Without align-

Figure I-2. *Phase by Phase Development of Key Ingredients for Effective IT Implementation*

Key Ingredients	Phase One Generating the Context for IT	Phase Two Designing an IT System	Phase Three Putting the IT System into Practice
Alignment	Vision aligned with business, organization, and technology strategies ⟶	System design aligned with vision ⟶	Operational use of system aligned with vision
Commitment/ Support/ Ownership	High organizational commitment; stakeholder support for IT ⟶	System designed to tap and promote user ownership ⟶	Users feel strong ownership for system
Competence/ Mastery	General task competence and IT literacy ⟶	System designed to use and promote mastery ⟶	Users mastering the system

ment, energy generated by system ownership and mastery can be misdirected and wasted. Without ownership, positive conditions of mastery and alignment may achieve incomplete, albeit appropriate, utilization. Without mastery, strong ownership and alignment may lead users to engage the system with enthusiasm and for the right purpose, but ineffectively.

MANAGING THE EXTENDED PROCESS

Though other conditions can promote effective implementation at various stages of the process, alignment, commitment/ownership, and competence/mastery are among the most influential. Hence, at each stage, an understanding of these conditions should guide implementation practices.

In the first phase, top managers want to ask themselves, "What actions will create a context that will ensure that new IT systems are aligned, owned, and mastered?" Executives can develop a vision aligning business, organization, and technology strategies—what I call the strategic triangle—and use it when evaluating systems proposed for their approval. They can work to improve the organization's general motivation and competence relevant to an IT-intensive future, for instance, by their guidelines for how middle managers ought to organize and manage work. And they can require consultative processes that generate support for IT systems in their formative stages.

In the second—the design—phase, sponsors and other participants can ask, "What concepts and processes will produce a sound system?" A theme of the design phase is the integration of the technological and organizational components of the IT system. They must be mutually adapted. The preferred process usually is one of parallel development of technology and organization, such that requirements or preferences regarding each can influence choices in the other.

Managers should evaluate the design options in terms of their likely effect on the motivation and competence of users. The effectiveness of advanced IT depends increasingly upon the internalized motivation and intellectual competence of users. New systems should help impart as well as utilize these social assets. Technology design elements that under the right circumstances can have the desired effects include wider access features and open- rather than closed-loop control functions. Organizational policies that influence commitment and learning include reward systems, supervising style, and selection criteria. These and other design elements need both to be mutually reinforcing and to produce behavior that is in line with the strategic rationale for the system.

Design processes must balance and integrate the expertise of systems specialists, organizational specialists, and users. User involvement helps to align the system with priority tasks, accelerates mastery and ownership on the part of those who are directly involved, and can increase support from the wider user community.

In the third phase, managers responsible for IT introduction ask: "How can we introduce and diffuse the system so that it is operationally aligned, progressively owned, and increasingly mastered by users?" Levers in this phase of the process include managers' actions—to involve users in planning the introduction and assessing the results of the system, to allow users to experiment with system capabilities, and to use the monitoring capabilities of the system to promote user learning and self-management. Managers' actions are important both for their concrete effects and for their symbolic meaning. How users interpret managers' intentions and the meanings they attach to the technology are crucial in determining which of the dual potentialities of IT are actualized: an organization based on compliance or one grounded in commitment.

This book addresses several key issues that cut across all three phases of the implementation process. One is timing: When do you address certain organizational design questions that are relevant to an IT system—in advance of the system design, during the design phase, or after operating the system? A second is user participation: Who should be involved, at what stages of the process, and for what purposes? A third issue is how to use assessments to evaluate and adjust the implementation process. An overarching issue is the role leadership plays throughout the process.

PURPOSE AND SCOPE OF THE THEORY

The theory I advance in these pages proposes relationships between certain outcomes and certain prior conditions. Insofar as practitioners value its economic and social outcomes and can influence its key ingredients, it is a practical theory. (My emphasis on theory as a tool for practitioners as well as a framework for further clinical research has led me to keep the theory as simple as possible, hence the narrowing of success factors to three key ingredients. Others, for example, Goodman and Griffith,[4] propose a more elaborate implementation model better suited to quantitative studies of the explanatory power of many factors.)

The theory is both comprehensive and selective. Unlike approaches that focus selectively, for example, on *content* (e.g., clarifying the organizational implications of IT), *contextual* factors (e.g., top management commitment), or *process* issues (e.g., prototyping and user involvement), this theory treats the materialization of IT content (the interacting social and technical dimensions of IT systems) as a process that occurs over time (before, during, and after system development) and in context (strategic, organizational, and political). The theory's selectivity lies in its identification of certain necessary, but not necessarily sufficient, contextual conditions, design considerations, and introduction factors. Its key ingredients do not include all the factors that may be important in a given situation.

Conceptual guidelines are offered in lieu of a complete catalogue of the actions and techniques that can influence the key ingredients. My larger purposes are to show how the framework developed here can be used as a tool for action planning and for diagnosing the strengths and weaknesses of implemented systems; and to illustrate some of the techniques that can be employed in the process.

OUTLINE OF THE BOOK

Part I, Chapter 1, analyzes the nature of the many relationships between information technology and organization. It helps define the implementation challenges that any proposed theory and practice of implementation must address. In Chapter 2, I present a specific case that illustrates the relationship between IT and organization.

Part II looks at the first phase of the process. It treats the generation of a positive context for IT development, including a broad vision to guide the development of IT (Chapter 3); organizational commitment and competence (Chapter 4); and broad and informed support for specific IT proposals (Chapter 5).

Part III analyzes the design phase, which includes design concepts that emphasize integration of organization and technology (Chapter 6) and a design process that involves users and multiple disciplines (Chapter 7).

Part IV focuses on the third phase, the process of putting the IT system into practice, including the introduction of complex IT systems (Chapter 8) and the diffusion of end-user computing (Chapter 9).

Chapter 10 concludes with a summary of the implementation process, and treatment of several major implementation issues that affect the mutual adaptation of organization and technology.

PART I—WHY IT IMPLEMENTATION MUST INCLUDE ORGANIZATIONAL CHANGE

The three-phase theory that I advance in this book rests on one very basic premise, namely, that the implementation of advanced information technology must include managing organizational change. This notion is crucial. Therefore, before we go through the three phases (which make up Parts II, III, and IV of the book), I want to show why the connection between information technology implementation and organizational change is immutable.

Chapter 1 attacks this point both evidentially—by reviewing systematic evidence of the adverse consequences for performance when IT is implemented without coordinated change in the organization—and analytically—by showing why organization and information technology are interdependent in many different ways. Chapter 2 makes the point illustratively—by describing how a retailer, Mrs. Fields Inc., attempts to use a carefully orchestrated combination of IT capabilities and organizational processes for competitive advantage.

Chapter 1—The Relationships between Information Technology and Organization—Crucial, Complex, and Manageable

As it is used in the workplace, information technology encompasses a rapidly proliferating array of hardware and software with the capacity to collect, store, process, and retrieve words, numbers, and images, to control equipment and work processes, and to connect people, functions, and offices both within and across organizations.

In the factory, IT embraces tools of manufacturing (e.g., robots, sensors, and automatic testing), material handling (automatic storage and retrieval systems), design (computer-aided design, engineering, and process planning), planning and control (manufacturing requirements and resources planning), and managing (decision-support systems). Implementations range from islands of automation or other isolated technologies to computer-integrated manufacturing systems that integrate design, manufacturing, material handling, and planning and control.

Office IT includes word processing, automated filing, transaction systems, computer conferencing, electronic mail and bulletin boards, video-teleconferencing, data-based inquiry programs, electronic spreadsheets, decision-support systems, and expert systems. This list is representative rather than exhaustive, meant to impart a flavor of the diversity of IT in the workplace.

The book is about information technology development and the organizations that employ IT. Certain ideas about organizational development are basic to my formulation of the IT implementation process. They are summarized in Figure 1-1.

Figure 1-1. Factors in the Development of Effective Organizations

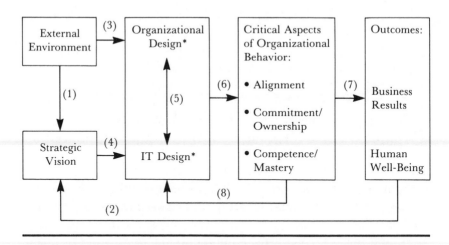

*Including design of *inter*organizational structures and interorganizational IT systems, e.g., allocating functions between manufacturers and their suppliers.

To be effective an organization must be managed as an open system, adapting its strategic vision in response to performance successes and failures and to such environmental factors as initiatives by competitors, changes in industry structures, and technical discoveries or inventions (see arrows 1 and 2 in Figure 1-1). The vision should embrace business, organization, and information technology strategies.

The company's formal organization and IT must be designed to reflect all components of the strategic vision and to take account of environmental factors, for example, regulations and labor markets (arrows 3 and 4). In addition, the organization and IT designs themselves must be matched and integrated (arrow 5). Virtually every element of work organization is either an integral part of an IT system or is affected by or influences technological aspects of the system. Job design, training requirements, organization structure, and decision-making patterns are among the more obvious organizational elements that interact with IT. But it is equally important to understand the relationship between aspects of IT (such as the type of work they automate and the information they generate) and organizational reward systems, measurement systems, and leadership styles.

Design choices about the formal organization and information technology are important because they shape organizational behavior patterns (the commitment and competence of employees and the alignment of their actions with the organization's priorities), which in turn affect business results and employee well-being (arrows 6 and 7).

A third consideration shapes the design of the organization and IT (the influence of environment and strategic vision were mentioned earlier). In making design choices, planners must anticipate and attempt to promote the particular pattern of commitment, competence, and behaviors which they believe will be instrumental to achieving the desired business and human outcomes (arrow 8).

Though I am getting slightly ahead of the story in what I am about to say, I frequently use the word "commitment," rather than the more neutral idea of "motivation," to refer to the general disposition of employees to do the organization's work. This word choice reflects a judgment that high commitment is increasingly a key ingredient for organizational effectiveness, especially in advanced IT environments. It is also in line with observed trends in industry.

Many top management perceive the human organization to be a potential source of competitive advantage (or disadvantage). As a result, we have begun to hear management philosophies and values articulated more clearly than ever before, and used to drive organizationwide transformations. Often these philosophies call for less bureaucracy—leaner, flatter organizations that emphasize some combination of greater initiative, innovation, participation, flexibility, and teamwork. Manufacturers such as Goodyear, Ford, and Cummins Engine are, for example, shifting away from "imposing control" and "securing compliance" and moving instead in the direction of "eliciting commitment." The issue of compliance-oriented versus commitment-oriented organization is now viewed as key, and IT planners are increasingly likely to be presented with high commitment or other explicit organizational ideals against which to plan an IT/organization system.

Several premises about IT and organization underlie the implementation approach proposed here. The first is that information technology and organization interact in ways that are increasingly crucial to the success of an IT system. The second premise is that advanced IT renders these interactions increasingly complex—influences are often mutual and subject to change over time. Coincidentally, and fortunately, the mutual relationships between organization and technology are becoming less deterministic as they become more significant and more complex. Thus, the third premise is that choices about the design and operation of IT systems can increasingly be guided by planners' preferences about organizational effects.

What evidence and analysis support these premises? And what are their implications for the IT implementation process?

LIMITATIONS OF TECHNOLOGICAL CHANGE—SOME EVIDENCE

The findings of several comparative studies drive home the point made earlier, that is, the successful exploitation of advanced information technologies requires changing the organization and its capabilities.

Researchers associated with the Massachusetts Institute of Technology (MIT) International Motor Vehicle Program analyzed a sample of five U.S. assembly plants that differed with respect to the amounts of technological and organizational change they had employed in their efforts to become world-class competitors.[1] Organizational reforms, where they occurred, took the form of participation mechanisms, flexible assignment patterns, multiple skilling, self-supervision, quality problem-solving groups, and similar policies designed to promote employee commitment and competence.

One GM plant in Massachusetts was typical of plants in which neither new work practices nor new technology had been introduced. A second GM plant, in Michigan, had been infused with $650 million worth of advanced manufacturing technologies, but had not undertaken significant organizational change. Two plants—a California plant of NUMMI (the GM/Toyota venture) and a Honda plant in Ohio—had coupled a moderate upgrade of technology with very ambitious work reforms. The fifth plant, Nissan's in Tennessee, was generally a little more technologically sophisticated but slightly less ambitious in implementing work reforms than the NUMMI and Honda plants.

Analysis of productivity and quality in the five plants led to conclusions that were arresting to the auto industry. Researchers found that the performance of GM's high-technology/no-work-reform plant in Michigan was not significantly better than that of its low-tech/traditional organization plant in Massachusetts. Advanced technology by itself seemed to make little difference. The NUMMI and Honda plants, with their moderate investments in technology but fundamentally reformed work organizations, dramatically outperformed GM's high-tech/traditional plant, assembling cars in about 45% less time and producing 45% fewer quality defects than the higher-tech plant. Nissan's slightly more automated but slightly less organizationally advanced plant had comparable quality but significantly lower productivity than the NUMMI and Honda plants. Again, the technology advantage appeared to be more than neutralized by a lag in organizational upgrading.

Advanced technology by itself seems unable to guarantee the kinds of significant performance advantages regularly delivered by technological innovation accompanied by work reorganization. Although these startling findings are drawn from a small sample of auto plants, many managers and other observers close to the industry believe that the conclusions reflect a general pattern.

In a second study that also stunned American manufacturers, particularly those in the metal-working industry who had pioneered the application of flexible manufacturing system (FMS) technology, Professor Ramchandran Jaikumar of Harvard found in American systems "an astonishing lack of flexibility compared with similar systems installed in Japan."[2] These technologies provide the flexibility to produce many different parts in small quantities at costs usually associated with high-volume production on single-purpose equipment. Comparing more than half of the installed systems in both countries (35 in the United States and 60 in Japan) that made products similar in size, complexity, and precision requirements, Jaikumar found that the average number of different parts produced on U.S. systems was 10 and on Japanese systems was 93. Also for every new part introduced into a U.S. system, 22 parts were introduced in Japan. Another indication that U.S. systems were failing to exploit the potential flexibility in the technology was the average annual volume per part, which was 1,727 for U.S. systems and 258 for Japanese systems. "The United States," Jaikumar concludes, "is not using [FMS] technology effectively, Japan is."[3]

Jaikumar attributes differences in U.S. and Japanese implementation of FMS to several factors: the degree of computer control incorporated in the system; the technical skill of the work force; and management approaches. By way of example, fewer than 25% of the technical work force in U.S. facilities had been trained on computer numerically controlled machines, while nearly all relevant employees in Japanese firms had this training. Similarly, U.S. companies invested only one-third the time devoted by the Japanese companies to upgrading skills. Practices that lead to low flexibility affect both the design and operating phases of FMS projects. A tendency for U.S. project teams to overdesign for flexibility often results in an arduous and often frustrating start-up process, following which operating managers and engineers assigned to maintain the system become excessively cautious, resisting practices that might utilize and expand the system's flexibility. Jaikumar contends that to achieve the flexibility inherent in FMS technology, American managements must provide for continuous process improvement through organizational learning and experimentation.

My own research in the shipping industry supports the conclusion that economic benefits of new technologies often depend on the implementation of a new organizational form.[4] Computer-based technologies and other technical innovations make it theoretically possible to operate ships with smaller crews. Engine-room remote sensing and control, automatic alarms, and automatic recording of operating parameters, for example, combine to eliminate the need for round-the-clock watch keeping in the engine room. New technology makes it possible to control engine, fuel, and navigation from the ship's bridge, enabling a single officer to perform functions previously distributed between deck officers and engineers. Comparing the records of technical and organizational innovations in the work systems aboard deep-sea vessels in the merchant fleets of eight countries, I found that to implement manpower reductions required versatile crew members and jobs with role flexibility. Role flexibility, it turned out, was acceptable in practice only when crew members could participate in the assignment process. Participation patterns had to be supported by practices that decreased the extreme social stratification of traditional crews. Thus, to utilize the new technology effectively, shipowners had to innovate socially as well as technically—they had to negotiate role flexibility with seafaring unions; modify maritime education programs to impart different skills; delegate management authority from shore to ship's officers; involve crew members in work planning aboard ship; and promote social integration among crew members.

A National Research Council (NRC) committee investigating "Implementation Practices for Advanced Manufacturing Technology" reached similar conclusions.[5] The committee, which I chaired, sent business executives, trade union officials, and academics to installations of advanced manufacturing technology in 16 firms, including Consolidated Diesel; Cummins Engine Company; FMC Corporation; Ford Motor Company; Frost Inc.; General Motors Corporation; Grumman Aerospace Corporation; Honeywell Information Systems, Inc.; IBM Corporation; Ingersoll Milling Machine Company; and McDonnell-Douglas Corporation.

Though the committee did not follow a comparative design in the spirit of the studies just cited, but selected, instead, many sites known to have implemented both organizational and technical innovations, the conclusion was clear—that traditional work organization is ill-suited to realize the potential of advanced manufacturing technology. The liabilities of the traditional organization derived from its hierarchical consciousness, detailed and fixed division of labor, and supervisory emphasis on the performance of the individual worker. New technology requires more assignment flexibility, more continuous learning, and more internal motivation than traditional work systems provide.

POOR COORDINATION OF IT DEVELOPMENT AND ORGANIZATIONAL CHANGE— SOME SYMPTOMS

The comparative studies cited above provide systematic evidence that implementing new technology without making appropriate organizational innovations often results in systems that fail to live up to expectations. Several examples will illustrate the range of symptoms of inadequate attention to the organizational aspects of IT systems.

Employees Ignore the System

Sometimes planners fail to provide the minimal organizational conditions required for an IT system to function. A case in point is a medical records and decision-support system introduced into several geographically dispersed clinics of a large medical care organization. Neither medical nor clerical personnel used the information system reliably. Doctors failed to enter diagnostic and treatment information from visits, which rendered the system's data unreliable. Because the system was unreliable, more and more people failed to use it. Ultimately, the system was removed. The system failed to meet its primary objective of providing instantaneous access to complete patient data, despite the fact that the computer system performed to specification.

Planners of the medical records system either had not anticipated or had neglected several organizational dynamics that proved to be crippling. The doctors' normal pace of work was so hurried that even minor additional retrieval and recording tasks were experienced as significant, and therefore were often neglected, even though the merit of the tasks was acknowledged. There was also a failure to take account of a location in a teaching hospital; the frequent rotation of doctors through units that did not have comparable procedures made it exceedingly difficult to develop and sustain the work habits required to maintain the system. In fact, the medical care agency had developed no organizational mechanisms to ensure system use, relying instead on voluntary use by traditionally independent doctors.

The performance of clerical personnel was also unreliable. Several factors undermined their perception of the importance of retrieving information for patients who came to the clinic. Previously, patient records had been used only rarely, and even after the new system was installed, as often as not there was no information on file for a given patient, since 40% were new each day. Finally, the clerks witnessed the doctors' own lack of support for the system. Efforts of the clinic administration to require system compliance were frustrated by the opposition of the union that represented the clerical personnel.

Low Morale among Employees

When a technical system deskills and demoralizes a work force, the system itself usually suffers as well. This happened to a telephone company that automated its geographically dispersed repair bureaus, employing advanced information technology to automatically test phone lines and monitor the status of repair orders.

This company reaped benefits and incurred costs from its implementation of advanced IT. Management benefited from the automation of time-consuming and tedious supervisory tasks, such as tracking case status and balancing workloads. Craft workers, on the other hand, experienced the automation of their tasks as a loss. The "testman," traditionally a "starched white shirt and tie" professional, is a dramatic example of this. Mastery of this job required both experience and considerable innate ability. The automation of the testing function made it faster, and radically decreased the value of the testman's accumulated skill, knowledge, and experience. As a result, testmen suffered psychologically, socially, and economically.

Other employee groups in the bureau were affected similarly, albeit less drastically, producing severe morale problems. Instances of sabotage occurred (e.g., a testman would cancel all information in the tracking system related to outstanding repair orders). The low morale and acts of sabotage in the repair bureau prevented management from achieving many of the potential benefits of a technically sound, advanced IT system.

Disappointing Results of System Use

Often results are less dramatic than suggested by the progressive degradation of the medical records system or the testmen's retaliation against the automated repair system. Results may be simply disappointing, a consequence of the potential inherent in the technology not being realized. This was the case with the Ace Company's decentralized order-processing system, which received inquiries from customers and salespersons, checked product availability, booked orders, and billed customers. Although the system succeeded in decreasing shipping times and errors, it simply didn't do what was really expected of it.

The Ace Company had not overlooked the human dimension. System development had included a major effort to educate primary users, particularly personnel in regional sales service centers, well in advance of the system's installation. But service center personnel did not operate the system on the planned "one-call" basis. Instead, they continued their prior practice of separating the jobs of phone contact and order-entry, complaining that the system's response time was too slow to check product availability while holding a customer or salesperson on the line. Moreover, separating the jobs the system was intended to combine accommodated personnel who preferred terminal work to phone contact and vice versa, and also enabled workers to avoid sharing a terminal. System designers had assumed that sharing a terminal was a simple social problem, which it was not at all in practice.

Planners also intended that sales personnel would describe the benefits of the system to customers, using it, in effect, as a competitive selling tool. This did not happen, either. Because they were denied direct access to the system, sales personnel were chagrined when they discovered they had become even more dependent on service representatives than before. In addition, because it did not accommodate certain exception pricing practices they believed were in the company's interest, sales personnel considered the system rigid. Moreover, they saw a radical alteration in the organizational pecking order—power shifted from the Sales to the Service Department, both of which were less powerful than the new Systems Group, which could define many of the procedures (e.g., exception pricing) and control the tools (e.g., terminals) Sales and Service used to accomplish their tasks.

THE COMPLEX INTERDEPENDENCE OF ADVANCED IT AND ORGANIZATION

Advanced forms of IT have broader and deeper organizational consequences than earlier forms. The greater the functionality of an IT system, the more levels of learning and adjustment are required to utilize it, ranging from operator skills through organizational procedures and structures to cultural fabrics.[6] Growing evidence suggests that progressive exploitation and integration of CAD/CAM increase the potential for further automation, the level of learning involved, the length of time required to assimilate the change, and the necessity that technological development be guided by a strategic framework.[7]

The batch systems that automated accounting functions in an earlier period reduced staff but otherwise implied relatively modest organizational change, for example, downgrading the skill requirement for data entry tasks. The introduction of on-line systems with broad databases, in which one system embraced several departmental functions, such as purchasing, accounts payable, and receivables, revised the relationship of each function to all the others. More employees were affected as users and recipients of information interacted directly with computer terminals.[8] Networking and distributed processing further increased the organizational and interorganizational scope of systems[9] and affected communication patterns in subtle ways.[10] Overall, IT possesses the power to integrate in new ways functions in separate organizations and in different steps in the value chain.[11]

Gibson and Jackson developed a matrix for mapping the benefits of IT—efficiency, effectiveness, and transformation— against their beneficiaries—the individual, functional unit, and entire organization.[12] The earliest forms of IT improved the efficiency and effectiveness of functional units, such as accounting departments. Advanced IT yields comprehensive benefits for the entire organization and transforms the activities of all beneficiaries (see Figure 1-2).

IT systems oriented primarily toward cost reduction often attempt to automate as completely as possible functions previously performed by individuals. IT systems oriented toward adding value (by increasing effectiveness or generating new products)

Figure 1-2. IT Benefit/Beneficiary Matrix

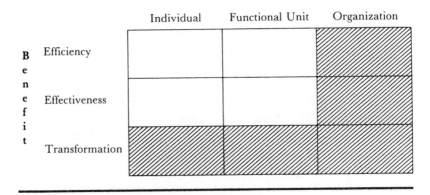

Note: Shaded cells of matrix depict range of benefits and beneficiaries of advanced forms of information technology.
Other cells were targets of earlier forms of IT.
Source: Reprinted by permission of the publisher, from THE INFORMATION IMPERATIVE by Cyrus F. Gibson and Barbara Bund Jackson (Lexington, Mass.: Lexington Books, D.C. Heath and Company, copyright 1987, D.C. Heath and Company): 28.

often emphasize a dynamic interaction between the technology and its users, including the generation of new information to be used in cognitively complex ways by the users. Zuboff has labeled these "two faces of intelligent technology" *automate* and *informate*.[13]

"Automate" describes "the application of technology that increases the self-acting, self-regulating, and self-correcting capacities of systems," "informate" "the application of technology that translates objects, events, and processes into data and displays that data." These contrasting capacities of IT can coexist in the same system; indeed, the informating capacity of a system often evolves from its automating capacity. McFarlan and McKenney cite an illustrative case involving the installation of electronic mail and word-processing systems to automate the preparation of bank loan paperwork.[14] Although conceived and introduced separately, the systems were functionally combined through the initiative of a loan officer and a consultant to facilitate decision making by loan managers. Headquarters and branch loan personnel could use the bank's electronic mail system to access an analytic tool for assessing loan performance contained in the word-processor-based loan system. Thus systems introduced to automate specific bank functions were reinterpreted to informate bank officers.

The organizational implications of informating technologies contrast sharply with the implications of automation.[15] IT designed to automate operations usually eliminates personnel, decreases the production system's dependence on the judgments of remaining personnel, and reduces the amount of training they need. Under these conditions, adequate performance can sometimes be achieved with close supervision and control-oriented rewards and punishments.

A contrasting organization is needed when IT is designed to provide operators with new information as a basis for upgrading decision making and the production of goods and services. For this type of IT to be effective, the organization and its human resource policies and practices must elicit a high level of spontaneous commitment, provide for higher-level cognitive skills, and cede considerable discretion and influence to those who operate the system. (The relationship between the requirements of informating technology and the motivation and competence that must be supplied by the organization is analyzed in detail in Chapter 6.)

The more companies compete on the basis of generating new goods and services or customizing existing offerings, the more obsolete the industrial bureaucracy becomes for utilizing IT.[16]

THE DUAL POTENTIALITIES OF IT

Two factors are converging to escalate the importance of knowledge about how to integrate IT and the organization. I mentioned them earlier. The first is that the relationships between advanced IT and organization are becoming more complex and more profound. The second is that they are, at the same time, becoming less deterministic. Organizational effects of the early big machine-based batch systems were relatively predictable—usually deskilling and pacing of work. Subsequent generations of IT have become less consistently associated with a given set of effects. The dual potentialities of advanced information technologies afford managements the opportunity to make choices about the type of organizational influence they want from the IT systems they approve.

By dual potentialities, I refer to the capability of the same primary technology to produce one set of organizational effects or its opposite.[17] The preferred approach of many companies to work force management is shifting away from a reliance upon imposed control toward active solicitation of employee commitment. IT can be a powerful force to either end. It can reinforce a control/compliance orientation or facilitate a move toward a commitment-oriented organization (see Figure 1-3).

IT is a powerful tool for control and compliance because it can monitor and record many aspects of behavior and performance. Providing these data to organizational supervisors strengthens their hierarchical control. The same technology can be used to empower lower levels of an organization by expanding access to information and extending it to more people. The empowering potential of the monitoring capability lies in its capacity to provide

Figure 1-3. Dual Organizational Potentialities

Compliance Effects	Commitment Effects
Monitor and control	Disperse power and information and promote self-supervision
Routinize and pace	Provide discretion and promote innovation
Depersonalize	Enrich human communication
Dispossess individuals of their knowledge	Raise skill requirements and promote learning
Decrease dependence on individual	Increase importance of individual skill and internal motivation

feedback to users in a way that drives learning and self-correction. The list of dualities goes on.

- IT can be used to routinize and pace operators' work or to increase operator discretion and provide a tool for innovation.
- IT can isolate and depersonalize or connect people and enrich the possibilities for human communication.
- IT can be used to dispossess and deskill individuals by building their job knowledge into the system, or to increase knowledge and skill requirements and impart users with a new understanding of their task and the factors that affect it.
- IT can decrease the organization's dependence on the skill and motivation of individuals in certain jobs, or increase the need for internally motivated and highly competent employees.

The case examples in subsequent chapters illustrate these dualities and others.

As IT itself becomes less deterministic, its effects depend increasingly upon precisely how the technology and the organization are configured and how the system is introduced and managed. The declining cost of computing power has combined with the increasing software-intensiveness of the technology to greatly expand the array of different technical solutions to a given business problem that management can consider. Because each of the possible technical solutions has its own set of organizational effects, organizational choice is broadened.

How planners regard the alternative organizational effects listed in Figure 1-3 will depend upon many factors. Planners must consider how these effects relate to the set of values or statement of organizational philosophy, if any, articulated by top management. Additionally, they must question whether these effects will, in practice, produce the levels of motivation and competence required by the evolving IT system. Given the purposes and requirements of the system, how important is it for users to be favorably disposed to the system and internally motivated to perform the tasks it requires? How important is it for users to be very competent? When the purpose and requirements of IT systems are served by higher levels of individual motivation and competence, it becomes more important to design and implement the system in a way that generates the effects listed in the righthand column of Figure 1-3. Conversely, when a generally compliant work force with modest skills can satisfy the requirements of a system, the effects listed in the lefthand column are, pragmatically speaking, more acceptable. In practice, most new forms of IT raise rather than lower the requirements for competence and internal motivation.

In each of the three broad phases of implementation, managers will make choices that determine which of the potential and opposite sets of effects is realized in any particular case. During the first phase management must decide which set best aligns with top management's strategic vision. In the second phase, planners need to decide which set of organizational effects will result in the best utilization of the technology, and design the system to promote those effects. They must determine, for example, who is to have access to the system and how the jobs of users are to be configured. In the third phase, they must decide how the system is introduced and managed, whether, for example, users are encouraged to experiment and invent. These activities contribute to the shaping of people's expectations of an IT system and the meanings they attach to it (e.g., whether they view it as a threat or as an opportunity). How people view the technology strongly influences how they utilize it.

DIFFERENT TYPES OF INFLUENCE BETWEEN ORGANIZATION AND IT

IT and the organization interact in at least seven different ways. Collectively, they explain why we cannot treat IT implementation without also discussing organizational change.

First, to be effective, an IT system may require new organization policies or designs, such as broader and more flexible jobs, a different distribution of authority, new training programs, or different selection criteria. The importance of this relationship was pointed up in the comparative studies cited at the beginning of this chapter. Planners obviously need to be able to plan these first-order organizational requirements at the same time that they plan the IT system.[18]

Second, the introduction of an IT system may elicit unanticipated organizational dynamics, such as new contests for power or status, altered patterns of communication, or more pervasive monitoring of behavior. The reactions of the testmen in the phone company repair bureau and the sales personnel in the order-processing scenario are illustrative. To the extent that they can anticipate such potential second-order consequences, planners can modify IT and organizational plans to offset unwanted effects and encourage positive ones, thereby increasing the overall effectiveness of the system.

Third, under certain organizational conditions, IT may itself be further elaborated and revised by users. We saw a minor example of this in the Service Center, where clerks modified the order-processing system to fit their personal preferences. Such influence by people on the technology is especially significant with end-user computing[19] and expert systems.[20] McFarlan and McKenney reported on a division of a large consumer products manufacturer that supplied Wang word processors, and a modest amount of training, to managers and administrative support personnel. The use of IT varied widely after four months. Of seven product managers, two had encouraged their support staff to "try it out," two had made systematic use of the word-processing features, and three had developed independent networks to support their sales staff.[21]

Fourth, IT may create or promote new organizational solutions. It may, for example, enable organizational members to work together across space and time, creating broader possibilities for the home-based professional.[22] It may also provide a means to circumvent the either/or choice between a centralized and decentralized structure by enabling managers to support the flexibility and responsiveness characteristic of a decentralized organization while achieving the integration and control of a centralized organization.[23] The Mrs. Fields case in the next chapter illustrates how IT can enable innovative organizational practices.

Fifth, IT can accelerate and refine organizational adaptations to changing conditions. Bruns and McFarlan report how IT allows early detection of, and response to, manufacturing problems; faster adjustments of incentives to serve sales programs; and better matching of recognition awards to the contributions of individuals or units.[24]

Sixth, IT systems and organizational forms can sometimes be considered as alternatives, in the sense that each is capable of performing similar functions, such as facilitating certain types of communication and coordination in an R&D department.[25] When planners understand the ways in which organizational forms and technology features are substitutable, they may consider a broader array of design options.

Seventh, planning an IT system can create opportunities for introducing organizational changes that management might view as desirable independently of the requirements or potential effects of the system. Managements have, for example, used IT planning as an occasion to set higher standards of excellence. This happened in a GE factory-of-the-future appliance plant; management formulated objectives for quality and inventory improvement that exceeded those enabled by the technology itself. GE also leveraged IT in the location decision for a flexible machining system (FMS) for aircraft engine components. Management placed the FMS at an established facility instead of a greenfield site only when the union agreed to a more flexible work organization. Although a flexible organization was required to operate the FMS effectively, management's objective was broader; it wanted to use the new work policies established as a pilot and precedent for similar changes throughout the work site. Thus the implementation of the FMS was conceived at every stage as instrumental to a broader organizational transformation.

Planners of the extended implementation process should be aware of each of these potential relationships between organization and technology. Otherwise they are liable to pass up opportunities to develop more effective IT systems or to be surprised by dynamics that undermine the ones they have introduced.

THE NEED FOR BETTER IMPLEMENTATION THEORY AND PRACTICE

The nature of the relationships between IT and organization has direct implications for the type of process we should employ to implement IT systems.

- The process deserves *priority attention and resources.* The crucial importance of managing the organizational aspects of IT systems warrants the direct attention of leaders and the commitment of organizational change resources, such as organizational consultation and education.
- The process must be an *extended* one, inasmuch as the key ingredients of IT effectiveness—alignment, ownership, and mastery—are influenced at various stages ranging from the conditions that exist prior to the start of system development to actions that take place after the system is in place.
- The process must be *inclusive.* Since the organizational effects of IT are often pervasive and the success of IT is dependent upon the support of many different groups, the implementation process should be encompassing in scope.
- The process should be *guided by organizational values.* In view of the dual organizational potentialities of advanced IT, the development of IT systems should be guided as much by a clear understanding of the preferred organizational effects of the system as by the business purposes it is intended to serve.

- The process should provide for the *parallel development of the technological and organizational aspects and requirements of IT systems.* Inasmuch as the actual interaction between IT and organization is two-way and changes over time, these two aspects of IT systems should be developed in parallel, if possible, and be mutually adapted.

An approach to implementing IT and organizational change that meets these criteria is outlined in Parts II, III, and IV.

Chapter 2—Relating IT and Organization— A Case in Point

The systems used by Mrs. Fields Inc. exemplify the growing complexity of the relationships between organization and IT. The company has made its mark in retailing by baking and selling cookies that are "fresh, warm, and wonderful and make you feel good," according to company CEO Debbi Fields. Debbi Fields leads the "people side" of the business, and her husband, Randy Fields, guides the analytic and strategic functions.

Our story of Mrs. Fields relates to two periods of the company's history.[1] First, we examine the role of the company's IT/organization strategy for the Mrs. Fields cookie stores as they grew from 2 in 1978 to over 400 in 1988. Second, we assess how a new business strategy emphasizing combination stores might affect the company's IT/organization strategy. Officially launched in 1988, the combination store strategy was built on the chain of La Petite Boulangerie (LPB) bakery stores acquired from PepsiCo the previous year. The combination stores are two to three times the size of the cookie outlets, and supplement cookie offerings with soup, sandwiches, and other bakery goods. They will carry the name Mrs. Fields Bakery Cafe.

Mrs. Fields had strong profits in 1986, reflecting a culmination of an impressive record of success in its traditional cookie store business. In 1987, company profits leveled off despite increased revenue, owing in part to difficulties encountered in certain overseas operations. In 1988, the company reported negligible operating profits and net losses, generating considerable interest in the financial press.[2]

Reflecting upon 1988 performance, Randy Fields stated that the company had a record year at the store level in the cookie stores part of the business. The strength of the cookie stores continued to confirm the commercial power of the approach to IT and organization which the company had developed over the past decade. Randy attributed the depressed financial results for the company as a whole to certain capital write-offs, and to other costs of the transition to the combination store strategy, which involved closing or retrofitting existing stores, opening new combination stores, doubling the size of the MIS staff, and retraining personnel.

THE COOKIE STORE PERIOD
OF MRS. FIELDS INC.

To assess the company's organization and use of IT during the cookie store business expansion period, we must start with competitive strategy. Two key factors essential to attracting and retaining cookie store customers are (1) a store culture that is strikingly upbeat, pleasant, and responsive and which customers immediately sense and appreciate, and (2) a product offering that meets the highest quality standards.

The challenging management task over the past decade for Mrs. Fields has been to continue to create and sustain the desired store culture and product quality throughout the rapidly growing system of stores. As one indication of management success in this endeavor, Randy cited fewer customer complaints per thousand purchases and fewer employees terminated for quality reasons in 1988 than eight years ago, when the company was a tiny fraction of its 1988 size.

Other factors have played a role in the commercial success of the cookie store. Like other retailers who sell perishable products to a walk-in clientele, Mrs. Fields cookie stores rely upon weekly, daily, and even hourly selling initiatives and careful management of stock. Reinforced by the successes of her first few stores, one of which she ran personally, Debbi Fields has strived to maintain the formula for good individual store performance as she has added more and more stores. This has meant sustaining high motivation among the hundreds of store managers and the thousands of employees. It has meant inculcating in each store innovative selling techniques and disciplined approaches to managing resources which are comparable to the ones she pioneered in her early stores. It has meant maintaining open channels of communication between the organizational top and bottom as the enterprise has grown from a few stores to dozens to hundreds. It has also required that management maintain the close integration of business functions—such as forecasting sales, ordering raw materials, and scheduling of store staff—that was easily accomplished when a few individuals personally coordinated them. Finally, managers at the top of the organization have needed to maintain a high level of knowledge about the specifics of store activities and, when necessary, to exercise control over them. The company's many geographically dispersed units and heavy reliance upon a predominantly young, inexperienced, and mobile (short-term) work force make this last point especially important.

The essence of the story about the cookie business is how advanced IT affected the organizational attributes just cited—employee motivation, selling initiative, resource discipline, two-way communication, functional integration, and monitoring and control—and how these functions in turn played a role in enabling Debbi Fields to influence store culture and product quality.

Communications Technology

Daily communication between Debbi Fields and her store managers is supported by two computer-based systems. PhoneMail answers the phone, and takes, stores, replays, and transfers messages. The system puts Debbi's voice into every store. It enables her to communicate ideas and concerns promptly and with nuance.

> If she's upset about some problem, Lui [a store manager in San Francisco] hears her sounding upset. If it's something she is breathlessly exuberant about, which is more often the case, he gets an earful of that too.[3]

PhoneMail is complemented by FormMail, which is accessed via personal computer. This system electronically sends and stores typed messages, which can be read at the convenience of the addressee. Debbi Fields and her store managers use this medium for more routine messages dealing with less acute issues. She nevertheless has a standing promise to reply, personally or otherwise, to store managers' messages within 48 hours. "On the morning I spent with her," observed a reporter visiting Debbi Fields's office,

> among the dozen or so messages she got was one from the crew at the Berkeley, California, store making their case for higher wages there and another from the manager of a store in Brookline, Massachusetts, which has been struggling recently. We've finally gotten ourselves squared away, was the gist of the note, so please come visit.[4]

These two messages—the Berkeley store crew making its case for higher wages directly with the boss, and the Brookline store manager inviting her to assess whether in fact the store had gotten its act together—are suggestive of the way the system enables upward influence. The nature and employment of these communications systems can make the organization feel flatter to its members than its relatively conventionally looking structure would suggest.

Programs for Store Management

IT assists management in managing numerous store-level functions. A program called the Daily Planner plays an integral role in the way store managers plan and replan each day's activities. Store managers enter a daily sales projection (based on sales a year earlier, adjusted by the store's growth factor), together with additional information requested by the program, such as the day of the week, whether it is a school day, and the weather. Richman reports how it works.

> Say, for example, it's Tuesday, a school day. The computer goes back to the store's hour-by-hour, product-by-product performance

on school-day Tuesdays. Based on what you did then, the Daily Planner tells him, here's what you'll have to do today, hour by hour, product by product, to meet your sales projection. It tells him how many customers he'll need each hour and how much he'll have to sell them. It tells him how many batches of cookie dough he'll have to mix and when to mix them to meet the demand and to minimize leftovers.

The computer revises the hourly projections and makes suggestions. The customer count is OK, it might observe, but your average check is down. Are your crew members doing enough suggestive selling? If, on the other hand, the computer indicates that the customer count is down, that may suggest the manager will want to do some sampling—chum for customers up and down the pier with a tray of free cookie pieces or try something else, whatever he likes, to lure people into the store.

On the other hand, the program isn't blind to reality. It recognizes a bad day and diminishes its hourly sales projections and baking estimates accordingly.[5]

The program does nothing the sales manager couldn't do manually, but it works faster and more reliably. It provides a better factual and analytical basis on which to make daily and hourly judgments. The store manager must still exercise his or her own judgments, not only in choosing which types of Mrs. Fields cookies to offer, but also in assessing the advice received from the Daily Planner. The manager must be able to recognize anomalies—when something is out of the ordinary. Then the manager's actions must take into account present circumstances that differ significantly from those on which the computer is basing its advice.

The computer also helps store managers schedule work-force levels. Managers enter daily sales projections for the next two weeks, and a scheduling program, based on Debbi's own baking and selling experience, projects an estimate of the number of people and the skills needed each hour. This estimate, which store managers use at their discretion, is generated in less time than it could be calculated manually.

IT also plays a role in the interviewing of applicants. The system evaluates the probability that an applicant will make a successful employee by reviewing, in light of the company's past experience, the applicant's responses to a series of questions presented on a display screen. The procedure does not necessarily save time, but it does supplement the store manager's subjective impressions with an objective assessment of other relevant factors. The choice remains the manager's.

Administration is abetted by, for example, generating a personnel folder for a new hire, placing the employee on the payroll, and reminding the store manager when an employee appraisal is due. It is expected that, in the future, the entire personnel manual will be on the computer, relieving store managers of the task of deleting old pages and inserting new ones. All of these functions conserve store managers' time without relieving them of any responsibility for managing people.

The computer also helps with the maintenance and repair of store baking equipment. A repair program leads store personnel through a diagnostic process when equipment breaks down. If this process does not yield a satisfactory solution, the computer initiates a request to have a vendor repair the equipment and automatically pays the vendor when the work is completed.

Several themes run through Mrs. Fields implementation of these store-oriented programs. First, the programs automate routine activities—data gathering, analysis, retrieval, and prompting—allowing store managers' time to be reallocated to selling and supervising store personnel. This is the payoff activity, according to Randy Fields: "In retailing the goal is to keep people close to people. Whatever gets in the way of that—administration, telephones, ordering, and so on—is the enemy."[6]

Second, the store-oriented programs can inform the store managers' actions in one of two ways: store managers can use the program's output as a point of departure for their own decisions, or they can use it as a substitute for making judgments. In theory the program would be used as a substitute for local decision making only by inexperienced store managers as they learned the business; and the programs would serve as an educative device during this period. Others would use it mostly to informate rather than automate decisions. Used this way, the system would neither interfere with a store manager's sense of accountability nor obviate his or her knowledge of the local situation.

Without more research, we cannot know how most store managers use the system. Both interpretations appear possible. Higher management could easily communicate a strong expectation that store managers follow program guidelines—and depart from them at their own risk. This latter possibility is suggested by Debbi Fields, in describing how difficult it was for her to delegate authority when the company began expanding.

> Management theory claims that it is wrong not to delegate authority to those who work for you. Okay, I'm wrong, but in my own defense, I have to say that my error comes from caring too much. If that's a sin, it's surely a small one. Eventually I was forced, kicking and screaming, to delegate authority, because that was the only way the business could grow.[7]

Other statements in her book support the idea that she was eventually able to let go. Randy Fields observed that most store managers experience these decision-related programs both as helpful on a day-to-day basis and as an educative device for improving their judgment about the matters covered by the programs. The fifth of the store managers who use the program the least, or who regularly ignore its advice, are also the managers of stores performing relatively poorly.

The third theme that runs through the store-level programs is that many of the analytic techniques and decision supports embedded in them are based on Debbi Fields's personal and successful experience in running one of her first stores. Take the idea of hourly sales goals:

> When Debbi was running *her* store, *she* set hourly goals. Her managers should, too, she thinks. Rather than enforce the practice through dicta, Randy has embedded the notion in the software that each store manager relies on.[8]

This pattern risks being experienced by store managers as intrusive, but we do not know to what extent, if any, this has been a problem.

Database Policy

Company policy at Mrs. Fields is to build all computer programs on a single database. Sales, raw material inventories, supplier invoices, payroll records, and utility charges all go into one database, eliminating duplication of data entry and placing a useful check on the growth and diversity of technology components. More important for the present analysis, a single database increases the ability of management to integrate all the functions supported by the computer. Eventually, the system will perform functions now performed manually, like checking current inventory levels against sales projections and ordering materials.

Store Performance Monitoring System

Mrs. Fields has developed a system that utilizes daily store and weekly inventory reports to monitor the details of store operations. Reporting to Randy Fields are seven headquarters managers, called "store controllers," who manage the monitoring of stores in specific geographical regions. This central control function is designed to free district and regional managers from the need to attend to minutiae, allowing them to concentrate on the people aspects of their jobs, selecting, developing, coaching, stimulating, and evaluating subordinates. Again, we can immediately visualize the dual organizational potentialities of the system. The managers responsible for the centralized monitoring system could readily transform it into a tool for achieving compliance, and thereby undermine other managerial efforts to promote store managers' commitment and initiative.

The Leveraging Effects of IT—And Its Other Potential Effects

The combination of programs that reflect Debbi Fields's approach to managing the business and the communications media that connect her with store managers has leveraged in a remarkable way her influence on store operations. Ideally, the systems permit her to exercise this influence while also developing the capacity of store managers to exercise business judgment and allowing the managers to do so.

Similarly, Randy Fields's store monitoring system has leveraged the capacity of a relatively few headquarters managers to track and analyze the quantifiable aspects of store performance and trigger corrective action. Ideally, the system does not undermine the commitment apparently fostered by Debbi Fields's line organization.

Given the susceptibility to differing interpretation of this IT—the communication technologies, store-oriented programs, and the monitoring system—it is extremely important for Debbi and Randy Fields to be clear and emphatic about their philosophical intentions regarding a compliance-oriented or commitment-oriented organization (see Figure 2-1).

The Store Managers' Role, Their Selection, and IT/Organization Systems

We have suggested that the IT/organizational systems employed by Mrs. Fields Inc. are potentially self-defeating if they are given a strong compliance interpretation. To estimate the business risks of this interpretation, we must analyze more closely certain aspects of the situation. The real risks appear to be reduced in this case by (1) the nature of the core tasks of store managers; (2) the way the IT/organizational systems relate to the core tasks and the central skills of store managers (or, to be more precise, the way they relate to them only indirectly, rather than directly); and (3) the types of individuals recruited for these positions.

There are two key aspects of running a store, according to Randy Fields.

Half of the tasks are based on human chemistry and the other half are numerically driven tasks. We hire store managers for the people tasks and we employ computer systems to ensure we do a rigorous job on the analytically based work. The systems also do as much of the routine administrative work as possible.[9]

Figure 2-1. *Dual Organizational Potentialities of IT Systems for Mrs. Fields Inc., Store Managers*

Types of IT and Their Primary Business Purposes	Potential Compliance Effects	Potential Commitment Effects
PhoneMail and FormMail		
Provide for fast and convenient two-way message flows	Experienced as intrusive and controlling	Experienced as opening up the organization; makes organization feel flat
	Increase dependence of store managers on Debbi Fields and her office	Increase amount of upward influence
Store Programs		
Save time that is redeployed to selling; provide reliably satisfactory decisions; decrease period required for new store manager to function; and leverage Debbi Fields's knowledge and experience	Substitute for exercising judgment; local knowledge not utilized	Aid to exercising judgment; local knowledge well utilized
	Remove incentive for expanding knowledge of the store business	Provide vehicle for learning about the business
	Undermine sense of responsibility for decisions covered by programs	Increase store managers' sense of being on top of all aspects of store and feelings of responsibility
Store Monitoring System		
Provides fast, detailed detection of problems along with prompt responses; relieves field management of minutiae.	Experienced as impersonal, pervasive, and punishing surveillance	Experienced as legitimate monitoring, and as allowing field supervision to increase the focus on people aspects of store

The most important point is that the programs do not automate, routinize, or control the *core tasks* of the store manager, which focus on producing a quality product, leading the selling effort, and creating the right store culture. They give as much guidance as possible about baking the product and provide timely prompters about the need for selling initiatives, but they do not relieve the store manager of full responsibility for choices in these areas.

The programs help the store managers create the right store culture, but exercise this influence only indirectly. Debbi Fields's communications leverage her influence on the thinking and motivation of the store manager, but how the manager then influences store personnel and shapes the store culture is a matter of his or her ingenuity and skill.

The company's strategy for recruiting and selecting cookie store managers is shaped by two factors: (1) the company's particular definition of its store managers' core tasks, and (2) the way it applies IT to other store-level activities.

The company is precluded from attempting to recruit the best all-around retail store managers because it cannot, in Randy Fields's judgment, pay the rates offered by fast food chain outlets that have four or five times more volume. Therefore, Mrs. Fields must emphasize a few attributes at the expense of others. Given the store manager's role, the company selects for enthusiasm, commitment, and people skills, and places less emphasis on experience, educational credentials, and analytic skills.

The design of the store manager's role—which relies more upon people skills and less upon knowledge of the business—makes the company less vulnerable to the high rates of turnover typical of retail store managers. In fact, Mrs. Fields's turnover of store managers has been trending downward.

In summary, the people emphasis of the store manager's role, and the selection of store managers for people/selling abilities rather than business judgment, ensure that the systems' strong guidance in the operational and analytic aspects of the business is less likely to be construed by store managers as intrusive or unduly controlling. This combination of role, selection, and IT support reduces the cost of turnover in the store manager position, and the good fit may actually help to decrease turnover.

Additionally, the fact that the IT/organization systems have been introduced into a new and growing company has made implementation easier. Almost all store managers have accepted the job and learned their role with the systems in place. Had they previously operated with greater autonomy, they might have been more ambivalent about the system.

THE COMBINATION STORE PERIOD

Debbi and Randy Fields intuitively knew that the store culture and product quality were important to their success in the cookie stores, but they did not fully appreciate the significance of these business assets until the 1987–1989 period, when they were assessing the new business strategy of offering a wider range of products. Recent market research had indicated that customers had high confidence in the quality of products of Mrs. Fields Cookies and would gladly purchase any of a broad range of products offered by the stores. The market researchers reportedly characterized the level of these findings as among the highest they had seen. Management reasoned that the consistently high quality of products, bolstered by the positive, upbeat purchasing experience, had created a strong brand name.

Management intends not only to continue to emphasize the store culture and product quality ingredients of the company's past success, but also to continue to extend the basic IT/organizational strategy analyzed above.

New programs being developed for combination stores are based on a growing understanding of their more complicated operational and selling tasks. Unlike the cookie store programs, which were based on Debbi Fields's personal experience in running her own two stores, the new combination store programs are being developed initially on the basis of specialists' analysis. Development will subsequently be influenced by the direct experience of members of senior management, each of whom plans to spend two months running a combination store.

Besides developing new programs to accommodate the differences between cookie stores and combination stores, the MIS group is developing expert systems to perform many tasks of middle managers and store controllers. The systems are being designed to observe what managers in these roles do, to detect patterns in managers' responses to problems, and then to relieve them of the need to produce that behavior. Randy Fields believes that the company's IT/organization systems are even more critical to its future success than they have been to its past performance. "I am betting the store on it—IT," he said.

So What?

Randy Fields believes that without IT, Debbi Fields could not have continued to project her influence throughout the expanding system and to know and control what goes on at the store level. In the absence of the unique and intricate ability of the technology to promote store-selling initiatives and maintain accountability for resources, the company simply could not have grown as dramatically as it has, at least not without resorting to franchising (which the Fields regarded as a less desirable business strategy). Finally, without a clear and consistent vision, none of the above would have been possible.

"Much more important [than the low percentage of sales spent on data processing]," Randy says, "is having a consistent vision of what you want to accomplish with the technology." He continues:

Imagination. We imagine what it is we want. We aren't constrained by the limits of what technology can do. We just say, "What does your day look like? What would you like it to look like?" If you don't have your paradigm in mind, you have no way of knowing whether each little step is taking you closer to or further from your goal.[10]

Mrs. Fields is a case in point in parallel development of information technology and organization guided by a strong business philosophy. The Mrs. Fields organization makes sense only with an understanding of its information technology, and the technology choices make sense only in light of Randy Fields's assumptions about the organization—its norms, and the abilities and motivations of Debbi, the store managers, and all of the managers in between.

BEYOND MRS. FIELDS

The Mrs. Fields case illustrates the importance and complexity of the relationship between IT and the organization, including the dual potentialities of IT systems. It also provides a basis for exploring more closely the interdependence of a number of choices in developing systems of the type employed by Mrs. Fields Cookies.

An example, which has many similarities to the Mrs. Fields case, will make the point. This organization had over a thousand retail outlets, each offering similar products and services, and each operated by a small staff.

Historically the organization had been highly centralized. Decisions about product offerings, displays, stock levels, pricing, and promotional and marketing activities had been made at several hierarchical levels above the store. Store personnel had been expected to be courteous, skilled at selling, and reliable and thorough in following prescribed routines.

Recently a new top management had undertaken to revitalize the organization, calling for more aggressive and imaginative initiatives by stores to bring in new customers and increase sales to regular customers. Authority and responsibility for decisions were to be moved lower in the organization, perhaps down to the store manager.

During the decentralization process, the company launched a major effort to develop an IT system that would support both the new business initiatives and the orchestration of the initiatives at lower organizational levels.

The author observed the managers and IT specialists of this company as they confronted a number of interdependent choices about precisely what business benefit to reach for, what technology to employ, how far to decentralize, and what skills to recruit in moving toward the future organization. Each choice depended upon assumptions about how other choices would be made.

Questions about business benefits, individual capabilities, organization structure, and technology, and about their interdependencies, are shown in Figure 2-2. These questions were raised during a meeting to review the status of the new IT system development. The discussion among systems developers, human resource executives, and line managers proceeded in the following manner.

Systems Specialist:

We can't continue in certain areas until we know more about the organization that will use the system. For example, we can't select

Figure 2-2. Interdependence of Business Benefits, Individual Capabilities, Organization Structure, and IT Development: Planning an IT System for a Retail Store Chain

IT Development	Organization Structure	Individual Capability	Scope of Business Benefits
What hardware, software, and operating rules will be required?	What decision-making responsibilities will be associated with roles that have different scopes of responsibilities: store, regional, divisional?	What can be assumed about analytic and business capabilities at store level, regional level? How much would it cost to recruit necessary capability at different levels?	What is the potential for more sophisticated analyses in our business?

the hardware and design the software until we know whether it should be designed to support decision making at store, regional, or division level. Who will be responsible for shaping local marketing initiatives? For controlling stock? For deciding prices?

Human Resource Executive:

As you know, we are feeling our way about how far to decentralize decisions in each of these areas. The extent of our decentralization depends in part upon how much your systems can provide guidance as well as data for making these decisions. Therefore, we need to know more from you about what you have planned.

How far to decentralize also depends upon what analytic capabilities and business knowledge we can assume we will be putting in place at the shop level and the regional level. What responsibilities can managers at these levels handle? We know that our present managers can handle more responsibility than we have given them in the past. But it is unrealistic to assume that they can call the shots on all aspects of their businesses, even with the support of new IT systems. We have discussed plans to recruit a higher caliber talent for store manager positions, paying as much as 60% more than our current scale. We need guidance from operational management about whether this makes business sense.

Line Manager:

I certainly cannot justify a 60% increase in the pay of store managers until we have done a better job of scoping the potential business benefits. The benefits depend in part on what the technology and the organization will permit us to do which we cannot do now. Moreover, I don't know yet what additional capabilities one can recruit for, say, 20% or 40% or 60% more pay.

And so it went. The participants were confronting the interdependence of business, technical, and social choices. The discussion is equally relevant to Mrs. Fields Cookies company, although it did not take place there.

POINTS OF EMPHASIS

Mrs. Fields and the other retail store example in this chapter help underscore and elaborate several points made earlier about the relationship between IT and the organization.

First, IT can be employed in imaginative ways, creating new organizational forms or processes. The use of FormMail and PhoneMail made possible a more personal connection between Debbi Fields and store managers than would otherwise have developed in an organization with so many outlets. The use of store programs to help simplify and support the analytic and administrative tasks made it possible to run outlets with managers who were for all intents and purposes sales managers. The monitoring system permitted a unique separation between the function of monitoring and controlling stores and the function of supervising them.

Second, many forms of advanced IT have dual potential consequences for the organization. The several IT systems in Mrs. Fields Cookies have not only direct business purposes, but also the capability to either strengthen the positive commitment of store managers or induce their grudging compliance. Thus, the case demonstrated how important it is for top management to clarify its philosophical preferences and intentions, and then continue to assess whether the systems are being used appropriately in practice.

Third, the intricate interdependencies of many forms of advanced IT and organization make it necessary for the design of each to take into account the design of the other. The store manager's role in Mrs. Fields could focus so strongly on the business priorities of upbeat atmosphere and quality product because store managers were supported by IT in other store management tasks. A change in any of these three elements—organizational design, business priorities, and IT functions—would require a reexamination of the other two. This point was made even more directly in the discussion centering on the second retail organization.

The extended implementation process examined throughout the rest of the book must be sensitive to these and other aspects of the relationship between IT and the organization.

PART II—PHASE ONE: GENERATING THE CONTEXT

Mrs. Fields's IT systems illustrated IT-organizational relationships. Although there is no systematic evidence on the point, the IT systems appeared to be well aligned and reasonably well owned and mastered by users. In any case the systems were up and running and were the product of an extended and ongoing implementation process. In Part II, we turn our attention to the first phase of that process (see Figure II-1).

The implementation task of the first phase is to create favorable contextual conditions, specifically strategic, organizational, and political contexts. These are treated in turn in the following chapters.

Formulation of a strategic vision capable of guiding both IT and organizational development is treated in Chapter 3. Chapter 4 analyzes the kinds of changes, particularly the development of employee commitment and competence, that can render an organizational context more favorable to IT development. Finally, Chapter 5 discusses issues related to generating broad and informed support for a proposed IT system. Notwithstanding the apparent logic of the sequence in which these topics are discussed, they can, and often do, occur in other sequences or in parallel. The important point is that these contextual factors collectively influence the alignment, mastery, and ownership of the IT systems that are developed within them.

Figure II-1. Phase-by-Phase Development of Key Ingredients for Effective IT Implementation

Key Ingredients	**Phase One** Generating the Context for IT	**Phase Two** Designing an IT System	**Phase Three** Putting the IT System into Practice
Alignment	Vision aligned with business, organization, and technology strategies	System design aligned with vision	Operational use of system aligned with vision
Commitment/ Support/ Ownership	High organizational commitment; stakeholder support for IT.	System designed to tap and promote user ownership	Users feel strong ownership for system
Competence/ Mastery	General task competence and IT literacy	System designed to use and promote mastery	Users mastering the system

Chapter 3—Creating a Strategic Vision

The issue is that incremental change will get you a ticket into day-to-day survival, but it won't get you a ticket for long-range survival. The only way I know to get at fundamental change is by creating new visions of the company, the organization, and its direction.

Archie McGill, a former AT&T executive whose stock in trade is change, continues:

The concept of a vision calls up very different images— something you are involved in, something you go home and tell your friends you are involved in, something you feel proud of, something you are passionate about.[1]

This chapter focuses on strategic vision—its components and the way they tie together. It also suggests the types of analysis and envisioning in which leaders must engage to produce a strategic framework. The underlying premise is that a well-conceived vision facilitates the integration of IT and the organization both in the system design process and when the system is up and running. The relationships among these factors are summarized in Figure 3-1.

The idea that the framework for guiding strategic choices should take the form of a "vision" has been broadly endorsed by thoughtful executives, academics, and consultants.[2] This vision takes the form of a broad conception of key aspects of the future enterprise—the goals it will pursue and how it will pursue them. The more compelling the vision, the more powerfully it will guide choices and motivate actions.

Figure 3-1. *The Role of Strategic Vision in Effective IT Implementation*

Action Levers	Strategic Context	System Design	System Introduction
Leadership, education, analysis, and visioning ⟶	Vision aligns broad business, organization, and IT strategies ⟶	Design integrates technical and organizational components of an IT system ⟶	System conforms in practice to strategic vision

THE STRATEGIC TRIANGLE

IT systems can take many forms, address a range of tasks, serve purposes of efficiency, effectiveness, or innovation, and have sharply different organizational effects. Thus IT development should be guided by a vision of the technologies the company will employ in the future in its plants, offices, and executive suites. This vision should comprehend the competitive strategy and organizational ideals that may drive or be driven by IT systems. IT should treat all three corners of what I call the "strategic triangle" (see Figure 3-2).

Figure 3-2. Strategic Triangle

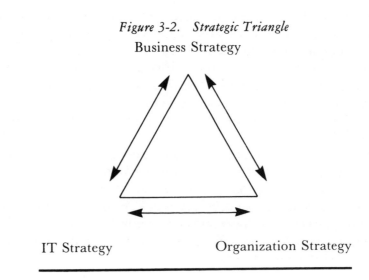

Business Strategy

IT Strategy   Organization Strategy

Consider some distinctions commonly made in each of these three domains. Michael Porter distinguishes among competitive strategies—low cost, differentiated product, and market niche. I employ a distinction between compliance-oriented and commitment-oriented organizations. Zuboff's differentiation between the automating and informing capacity of IT is an example of a distinction among IT strategies based on technological capability.

Our understanding of how choices in one area of strategy relate to choices in other areas has developed over the past two decades. The first to be clarified was the business strategy–organization connection. Since Alfred Chandler's seminal study of strategy and structure,[3] we have gained progressively more knowledge about how organization structure, systems, and skills can be tailored to support a chosen business strategy and, conversely, how existing structure and other established aspects of an organization can constrain or shape business strategy.[4] For example, a strategy of adapting competitive behavior to local conditions is matched by delegating authority and developing competence at lower organizational levels. Another example is that a business strategy requiring a stream of product or process innovations is better served by fluid and flexible organizational forms than by segmented and tightly bounded organizational units.[5]

The business strategy–technology relationship began to receive attention in the late 1970s, as academics and managers came to recognize that process technology, including advanced IT systems, must address key success factors[6] and, conversely, that new capabilities of advanced IT could influence the choice of business strategies.[7] We can, for example, support a low-cost strategy by combining automation and MRP systems that increase equipment utilization and reduce inventory-carrying costs and accounts receivable. A differentiated product strategy, on the other hand, is better supported by a CAD/CAM system that facilitates product customization and decreases lead time to new product development.[8]

The remaining relationship—between IT and organization—was recognized in the business literature later, and less systematically, than the other two. It is the primary concern of this book. Already, in Chapter 1, we explored the many forms interaction between IT and organization can take. The dual organizational potentiality of IT is especially important. Whether an IT system promotes a compliant organization or a committed one often depends upon certain technical choices (as between closed-loop and open-loop features) and management actions (as between using the monitoring capability primarily for control or for learning). To choose appropriately among these alternatives, management must decide how important it is for the work force to be committed rather than merely compliant.

Distinctions among strategies in all three domains are here broadly construed. Actual strategies are more detailed, specifying, for example, how product differentiation is to be achieved, how commitment is to be promoted, and how information technology will be utilized generally. A strategic triangle sanctioned by top management would guide not only the acquisition and development of IT, but also the methodologies for approving and assessing it.

In this chapter, I relate the search for alignment by the managements of four companies, and suggest the role the strategic triangle can play in IT development.

INTERNATIONAL METALS, INC.—GETTING ITS TECHNOLOGY ACT TOGETHER

Dean described and analyzed a sequence of management actions for International Metals, Inc. (IMI) which produced a new IT strategy, one responsive to previously established business and organization strategies.[9] Establishing the new IT strategy also moderately improved the climate for IT development and generated the necessary support to launch two projects. Instrumental activities included creating policy formulation groups; forming a steering committee comprised of many stakeholders; visiting other companies; soliciting consultants' views about different IT strategies; and promoting dialogue between the managers who were proposing the new IT strategy and the senior executives who would have to approve it.

Initially, IMI lacked a strategic vision incorporating approaches to external competition, technology, and organization. Top executives were committed to decentralization into business units, presumably to increase the cost-consciousness of middle-level managers and enable them to adapt to the unique competitive pressures faced by their businesses. The approach to IT was neither related to this business/organization strategy nor made explicit. Past IT strategy was nonetheless implicit in the allocation of computing resources; two-thirds were devoted to business computing (e.g., accounting, payroll), one-third to manufacturing operations (e.g., process control), and none to the integration of manufacturing and business systems (e.g., CIM).

IMI's organizational climate was at first decidedly inhospitable to IT implementation. Upper levels of the organization were very unsophisticated technologically, the corporate culture was risk averse, and the planning time perspective was short term. The organization was also segmented. Each function and each business went its own way and attended to its own priorities. In 1978, management formed an R&D planning group to encourage IMI's R&D and business units to think both long term and strategically. In 1982, it created a strategic technology group to help business units incorporate consideration of technology into their business plans. The executive committee, with the involvement of corporate planning and the new strategic technology group (which reported to the vice chairman), drafted a Statement of Direction that included a call for technological innovation.

The strategic technology group devoted considerable attention to computer-based technologies. Visiting other companies that used IT strategically, its members were struck by the range of applications they found, applications that went well beyond the business applications emphasized in their own company. In April 1983, the head of the group organized a three-day meeting between top-level representatives of three corporate areas—MIS, process computing, and research—and two computing professionals from business units to "deal with what IMI should do with computers." Invited to offer advice on how IMI should use computer technology, representatives from IBM, Digital Equipment Corporation, General Electric, and Arthur D. Little urged the company to emphasize the previously neglected areas of manufacturing processes and computer integration of business applications and manufacturing. By the end of the meeting, IMI participants had reached consensus on a computer strategy for the next decade that emphasized computer-integrated manufacturing. The group not only made headway on a technology strategy, it also improved the climate for IT development by lowering some organizational barriers. Observed one participant:

> You've got four computing communities in the company: the research group, MIS, the process computing group, and the plants. To get anything done, those four end up having to coordinate and work together. The overlap had been minimal, and the interfacing had been only when necessary. The thing that's getting increasingly apparent to everyone is that . . . we've all got a vested interest [in CIM], let's work on it together.[10]

When first presented to a subcommittee of the executive committee, the proposed IT strategy, including a request for pilot CIM projects in one or more business units, was not well received. Indeed, the presenters felt "blown out of the water." Executive committee members had interpreted the proposal as running directly counter to their effort to decentralize the corporation. As one presenter acknowledged:

> Those of us who had considered computerization had never dealt with the question of whether or not computers should be used in a centralized or decentralized corporation. . . . You can draw the corporate lines either way. . . . But when we were talking about words like "architecture" and "networking" and so on, people thought that meant centralization at a time when they were trying to be decentralized.[11]

According to another presenter, it was their identity as members of corporate staff as much as their words that had raised concerns about alignment of the proposed IT policy with the existing decentralization strategy.

> They wanted no inference whatsoever that the integration effort was going to centralize. . . . Maybe, if we could have had a represen-

tation from the two or three major business units with us as presenters, the officers would not have read what they read into it.[12]

The IT strategy statement was subsequently revised to recognize explicitly the need to respect and reinforce the concept of business unit autonomy. At a second meeting, the executive committee approved the IT strategy and gave the computer spokespersons a green light to go to the business units.

Two business units sponsored computer-integrated manufacturing projects, but with differing implications for the developing corporate consensus on IT strategy. One division undertook a CIM project drawing upon available corporate engineering resources, contributing to the learning of both division and corporate staffs. However, a second division launched a CIM project marked by animosity between the division and the Corporate Process Computing Group. Thus, the political progress made in pulling together different IT constituencies in IMI was at once both significant and far from complete.

AT&T IN THE EARLY 1980s—
DISCONNECTED STRATEGIES

A well-developed statement of business, technology, and organization strategies and their interrelationships is today the exception rather than the rule. Examination of a company's strategies, whether explicit or implicit, often reveals contradictions. AT&T in the early 1980s, when striking discrepancies had developed between two corners of its strategic triangle, is a case in point.

AT&T's business strategy, though it didn't ignore concerns about cost, placed far greater emphasis on quality of service to customers. Satisfied customers directly fulfilled one of AT&T's missions, and helped the Bell operating companies deal with public rate-setting commissions.

A pioneer in the application of information technology in its U.S. operations, AT&T addressed the business-technology connection systematically. Maintaining the integrity of the network—

the remarkable capacity for any part of the phone system to be connected to all other parts—was key to its technology strategy. This strategy involved the coordinated development of different pieces of equipment and their uniform applications throughout the system, which produced continual improvements in service. AT&T's IT strategy also called for successive generations of increasingly automated and reliable equipment. Reliability directly supported quality of service (albeit at a cost that had to be reexamined when the 1984 breakup of AT&T and partial deregulation of the industry subjected its parts to more cost pressure). To the extent that it reduced the size of the work force, automation diminished the importance of the human factor as a source of variance in system performance. But AT&T's IT strategy also included the development of administrative systems to help manage the large work forces that dealt with customers and maintained equipment. These systems, which automated such supervisory functions as assigning work to employees and monitoring their performance, were intended to promote both efficient use of human resources and more reliable performance, including service. Thus, AT&T's technology strategy was directly correlated with its business strategy.

AT&T also attended to the business strategy–organization connection. National attitude surveys of AT&T employees in the late 1970s and early 1980s convinced top management that growing disaffection threatened the corporation's ability to maintain high-quality service. Working under the assumption that a work force satisfied with the way it was treated would be more likely to want to satisfy customers' needs, management articulated a commitment to change the style of AT&T managers. More listening and greater consideration of employee concerns were to become hallmarks of the new management style.

At the same time, Communications Workers of America (CWA), which represented the majority of AT&T workers, was coming under growing political pressure from its members to do something about increased "job pressure." In the 1980 contract, union and management agreed to establish quality-of-work-life (QWL) mechanisms that would involve employees in solving work environment problems that affected them and the quality of service. Joint technology review committees were established in all the operating companies to review new technology prior to its introduction. Though it would take time for the effects of these changes to be seen, a new organizational vision was beginning to take shape. Like the technology strategy, this vision was correlated with the company's service-oriented business strategy.

AT&T had drawn two-thirds of its strategic triangle. But the remaining leg, the line that would have completed the connection between technology strategy and organization strategy, remained disconnected (see Figure 3-3). Automation continued to generate

Figure 3-3. AT&T in the Early 1980s: Misalignment of IT and Organization Strategy

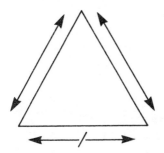

Business Strategy
Service emphasis

IT Strategy
Network integrity
Automation that
    deskills and
    routinizes jobs
Automated supervisory
    functions that monitor
    and pace workers

Organization Strategy
Considerate management
Participation and involvement
    (The deskilling and monitor-
    ing nature of the IT systems
    tends to create depersonal-
    ization and powerlessness
    rather than promote the
    consideration and involve-
    ment called for in the newly
    espoused organization
    strategy.)

employee anxiety and actual dislocations that hindered management's attempt to create the desired climate. Automated equipment continued to deskill and routinize jobs, decrease employee motivation, and even trigger sabotage of new equipment (recall the alienation of repair craftsmen reported in Chapter 1). The new IT-based work force management systems were especially offensive to the work force, which resented the constant surveillance and unrelenting pace of their work.

The contradictions between the control and compliance effects of technology and the new organizational philosophy of commitment caught the attention of a few AT&T executives. They began to formulate organizational criteria for new work technology in Bell Labs and the central AT&T departments. This effort to address how the quality of jobs and the centralization-decentralization of decision making should be considered in the specifications for new technology never gained sufficient momentum, and did not survive the breakup of AT&T. Nevertheless, the regional telephone companies have in recent years exhibited more conscious attention to the alignment of some of their IT systems with the organizational reforms initiated by AT&T and the CWA in the early 1980s.

EASTMAN KODAK'S MRPII
SYSTEMS—SEARCH FOR ALIGNMENT

The experimental search for strategic alignment is well illustrated by Eastman Kodak. Increasingly severe competition in the early 1980s prompted Kodak's top management to rethink the company's product market strategies, organization, and information systems.[13] In 1985, Kodak was reorganized into some two dozen business units, each focused on a specific market segment. At about the same time, CEO Colby Chandler articulated a new culture intended to promote customer orientation, nurture innovation and change, allow delegation of decision making, and encourage risk taking.

Kodak traditionally made everything it sold in a highly integrated manufacturing function. Following the reorganization, business units were encouraged to make active make-or-buy decisions, and some began to switch from Kodak to outside suppliers. Kodak's manufacturing executives expected decentralization to help units isolate relevant costs for make/buy decisions and increase their ability to compete with external sources.

Manufacturing units found that the centralized MRPII system recently installed to meet the requirements of a fully integrated manufacturing system was inappropriate to the newly decentralized organization. Management began development of decentralized MRPII facilities in 1986, using a self-contained plastic injection molding department (Department 23) as the first pilot. Department 23 had lost much of its Kodak business, and it was attempting to build an external business for plastic parts. Consequently, it needed to be able to deal effectively with a greater number of different products in smaller volumes, as well as manage its traditional business better.

Department 23's MRPII system was, by all accounts, a success after six months. The system improved on-time delivery performance, decreased procurement lead times, and more accurately identified item costs. MRPII helped department managers establish priorities and facilitated timely identification of problems. It was also an important educational device, requiring and enabling department personnel to better understand the nature of the businesses they were responsible for. Department 23's MRPII system, and the organizational changes that accompanied its implementation, reinforced ownership and entrepreneurship—key objectives of the decentralized structure. Kodak's decentralization of manufacturing had influenced the choice of IT, and the pilot implementation of IT had, in turn, enabled and reinforced the company's decentralization strategy. In combination, organizational change and new IT promised to serve Kodak's economic objectives.

Successful as the pilot implementation was, serious questions arose about the system's appropriateness for other departments and for the larger manufacturing organization. Because the microcomputer-based MRPII was not tied into a larger IT system, others who might have been able to make use of it did not have ready access to it. Moreover, many manufacturing departments were less autonomous than the pilot department. Given the perceived need for an MRPII system that would cover larger segments of the total manufacturing organization, a debate ensued about the relative merits of minicomputers embracing the information needs of larger segments and more hierarchical levels of the organization and microcomputers focused on the local needs of the individual departments.

The technology and organizational choices open to Kodak are shown as a matrix in Figure 3-4, with coordinated choices located on the diagonal. Kodak's late 1980s solution appeared to reside in some combination of departmental- and intermediate-level sys-

Figure 3-4. Eastman Kodak's Options in Designing MRPII Systems and the Manufacturing Organization

TECHNOLOGY CHOICES	Centralized organization to coordinate and optimize total manufacturing	Intermediate levels of decentralization	Decentralized organization to foster local accountability and initiative
Departmental MRPII Systems (Microcomputers)	Mismatches — Would fail to provide information to authorized decision makers, e.g., in headquarters		Department 23 MRPII reinforced autonomy of department
Intermediate-Level MRPII Systems (Minicomputers)		Minicomputer-based MRPII systems would match intermediate level of decentralization	Mismatches
Central MRPII Systems (Mainframe computers)	Earlier single MRPII system matched the centralized organization, at least in principle		Would fail to provide information to authorized decision makers, e.g., in departments

ORGANIZATIONAL CHOICES

tems. Off-diagonal cells in the matrix illustrate how systems that are poorly matched to the organization either deliver information to people who can't use it or fail to deliver information to those who need it.

The Kodak example underscores a key element in managing alignment—parallel design processes. Although Kodak management had moved to decentralize, it was still working out the balance between departmental autonomy and interdepartmental coordination, while a parallel process was attempting to identify the most appropriate IT system.

Ideally, the technology and organizational design processes should interact. A creative solution to the need for both local information processing and organizationwide communication might, for example, also help to resolve organizational design dilemmas.

THORN EMI HOME ELECTRONICS INTERNATIONAL—ALIGNED STRATEGIES

Management at Thorn EMI Home Electronics International (THEi), a service company in the United Kingdom, is very conscious of the need to align all three corners of the strategic triangle. Though it is too early to judge the success of a major IT development effort there, the strategic framework within which development and implementation are taking place is instructive.

THEi rents home entertainment equipment in the United Kingdom and 21 other countries. In the United Kingdom, where a significant percentage of home TV sets are rented, THEi had more than 1,100 stores in 1987.

The U.K. business had been extremely profitable, from the time THEi first introduced black-and-white sets through its later introduction of color TVs, VCRs, movie cameras, and videotape and complex audio equipment. THEi's performance began to decline in the mid-1970s as relatively more reliable and less expensive products encouraged more potential customers to buy instead of rent. Rental business managers had meanwhile become complacent, neither revising their organizational practices, which had been shaped during a seller's market, nor reforming their systems and administrative procedures, which were geared to collecting and accounting for cash receipts, not to marketing and enhancing the service performance. Terminations began to outnumber new rental contracts, and the subscriber base showed a steady decline.

In 1983, Jim Maxmin was appointed head of THEi with a mandate to revitalize the business. Maxmin first revised the business strategy. In pursuing a strategy that maximized cash flow and provided minimum investment in stores, service facilities, and rental stock, management had accepted the inevitable erosion of THEi's subscriber base. Maxmin's new strategy called for investment— both to stabilize and then augment the subscriber base, and to increase the number of rental items per subscriber. It shifted emphasis from administrative controls and cost reduction to marketing and service. Maxmin envisioned each store analyzing local opportunities for growth and targeting selected market segments through telemarketing and direct mailing initiatives.

Maxmin articulated an organization strategy that was consistent with both the new business strategy and his personal philosophy. His mission statement called for

> an organization structure that operates with a decentralized, open management style which ensures the organization has a minimum of hierarchy and limited spans of control. This organizational design . . . will ensure flexible, responsive operations, encourage good communications, and promote teamwork rather than policing.

Implementation of Maxmin's business and organization strategies was well under way by 1987. Management had invested new capital in the business, removed many layers of the organization, and pushed decision-making responsibility down the hierarchy. This not only stabilized the subscriber base and increased revenues and profits, but also, surprisingly, improved cash flows. Managers began to perceive more clearly the enormous potential of further development, and the inadequacy of existing information tools for managing the business. Maxmin's mission statement had recognized this deficiency. "Systems and information technology," he wrote, "will be employed to help provide differentiation and competitive advantage in our markets, ensuring that the MIS drawing on these systems will provide accurate, timely, and actionable information geared to individual accountability."

New systems needed to be everything THEi's past computer-based systems were not—flexible, integrated, and designed to assist local initiatives rather than serve as vehicles for central control.

Figure 3-5 summarizes the shifts that created a new strategic

Figure 3-5. Thorn EMI Home Electronics International: Old and New Strategic Alignments

Business Strategy

From an emphasis on administration
and cost reduction
to an emphasis on marketing,
service, and growth

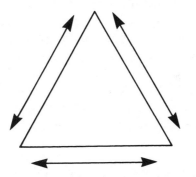

IT Strategy
From an emphasis on control,
administration, and cash
accounting
to an emphasis on decentralization, commitment, and
value-added business activity

Organizational Strategy
From a centralized,
compliance orientation
to a more decentralized,
commitment orientation

alignment between business, organization, and information technology at THEi.

Management developed an analytic model of the rental business, and undertook to design, on the basis of this model, information systems to support a variety of activities, including telesales and marketing, order processing, payments processing, stock control, arrears control, and service scheduling. Prototypes of several of these systems were being implemented in 1988.

Despite his prescription for new information technology, Maxmin perceived actual system development effort to be guided by past practices rather than concepts appropriate to a decentralized and market-oriented business. In the summer of 1987, he decided to increase the priority given to system development.

Maxmin contracted with consultants to help develop his management team's understanding of the implications of the business and organizational strategies for IT system development. He arranged for a case study to be written on the company's most relevant prior experience, the Kendal project (reported in Chapter 8). The case, which illustrated the costs of failing to integrate IT, organization, and business priorities, triggered a review by THEi executives of their present and planned IT systems efforts and an exploration of options in design features and other implementation tactics. The result was not only a clarification and reaffirmation of the IT vision, but a step toward broader and more informed support for THEi's strategic objective of automating and informating its stores and service centers.

TOWARD BETTER STRATEGIC VISIONS

Though top management usually has a relatively clear business strategy, it often lacks anything that could pass for a conscious and coherent IT or organization strategy. Management's strategic thinking about IT is usually the least developed, and the cases presented in this chapter are typical in this respect. Recall that top management at both THEi and Kodak had only recently developed IT strategies. A survey of 80 CEOs and corporate presidents found that only a minority took an active, positive stance toward

IT, and top managements who advocated IT did not necessarily have a *strategic* view of it.[14] A more encouraging trend in line management thinking about IT is reported by Rockart.[15] Sampling a management group that included younger middle managers, Rockart found line managers taking an increasingly active role in the conception and implementation of IT systems. Given the complex relationship between advanced IT and organization structures and processes, *only* a line manager has the power and perspective to initiate and execute required organizational changes. The larger importance of IT to business should warrant top management's direct involvement in the formulation of IT strategies.

Even when top general managers view business, organization, and information technology strategically, they may fail to think through how each strategy relates to the other two. AT&T, for example, had conscious strategies at each corner of its strategic triangle but failed to make the connection between its organization and technology strategies.

Lack of strategic alignment is explained partly by the recent recognition of IT's strategic role. But organizational factors also play a role. Top line managers must rely upon a different staff group to assist them in each of three areas. They turn to planning groups for help with business strategy, IT specialists for assistance in allocating resources for IT systems, and human resource departments and organizational consultants for guidance in organizational planning.

I can suggest several types of remedies for strategic misalignment. Seminars or workshops for top line managers can raise their awareness of the interrelationships among the choices they are making or need to make. Bringing together CEOs with members of their top management team to discuss selected case histories of alignment and misalignment and concepts about the potential connections between IT and organization can help energize top management to develop and communicate a strategic vision.

The existence of a comprehensive statement covering each of the three strategies and their interrelationships is less important than the organization's commitment to the mode of thinking such a statement represents. Everyone who is responsible for sponsor-

Figure 3-6. Statement of Organizational Impacts of IT

First-order organizational consequences of technical system	MAY LEAD TO	Forecasted second-order human consequences of technical system and organizational changes
Employment Effects Staffing level requirements		Job security or insecurity
Job Level Impacts Skill requirements—level and type		Job enrichment or job improvement
Job specialization—type and degree		
Operator functions augmented or eliminated		Remuneration—increased or decreased
Increased individual discretion versus routinization of work		Status gains or losses
Clarity of job purpose enhanced or decreased		Career optimism or pessimism
		Sense of mastery or lack thereof
Nature of work—abstract or concrete		Involvement gains or losses
		Understanding of relationship of own work to whole task
Human engineering features of electronic equipment		Safety—health hazards
Structural and Procedural Changes Decentralization versus centralization		Sense of autonomy versus external control
Definition of accountable unit size		Self-supervision increased or decreased
Dependencies between positions and units		Problem-solving orientation versus "game playing"
Amount and type of performance measurement, feedback, and overt control		Ownership of goals and sense of accountability—higher or lower
Spans of supervisory control		Reinforcement—more or less
Number of hierarchical levels		Job pressure—optimum or too little or too much
Size of organizational unit		
Face-to-face communication requirements		Perceived equity—greater or lesser
Impact on Flexibility Constraints on work schedule		Compatibility or tension between work and nonwork requirements
Constraints on physical movement and social communication		Sense of community or fragmentation
		Social satisfaction or social isolation
		Personal versus impersonal climate
Information Impacts Availability of business data		Learning promoted or not
Availability of personal data		Privacy protected or invaded

Source: Richard E. Walton and Wendy Vittori, "New Information Technology: Organizational Problem or Opportunity," *Office: Technology and People,* Elsevier Science Publishers, Physical Sciences & Engineering Division (1983): 266.

ing, developing, introducing, and operating IT should be clear about both the company's strategic business priorities and its organizational ideals. They should engage in dialogues with others in the organization to clarify the potential implications of a proposed IT system for the business and the organization, and vice versa. THEi's experience shows that top management's articulation of a set of coordinated strategies is not sufficient. Despite the aligned strategies that existed in the chief executive's thinking and on paper, the individuals responsible for the experimental project installed an IT system that neither addressed the new business priorities nor promoted the new organizational preferences. Precisely how this project got off track will be analyzed in Chapter 8. The point here is that management did not take steps to ensure that developments were consistent with the strategic vision.

Top management should require sponsors of a new IT system to do their homework. This is the spirit of a device outlined by Walton and Vittori—an organizational impact statement that details the first-order changes planned to implement the IT and that forecasts its second-order human consequences (Figure 3-6).[16] First-order consequences include degree of abstraction of work, amount of decision discretion, and pattern of dependency among units. Potential second-order consequences include emotional reactions and informal behaviors by individuals in response to changes in their jobs and organizational positions. The requirement to "file" an actual statement is probably unnecessarily bureaucratic in most circumstances, but top management should insist that planners engage in the organizational planning and forecasting that such a statement would entail.

Chapter 4—Promoting Organizational Commitment and Competence

A National Research Council committee observed that companies involved with advanced manufacturing technologies tend to intensify their pursuit of the following objectives:

- a highly skilled, flexible, problem-solving, and committed work force;
- a flexible, humane, and innovative management organization with fewer levels and job classifications;
- a high retention rate of well-trained workers; and
- a strong partnership between management and labor unions— where unions represent the work force.[1]

The committee further observed that these objectives, which were initially driven by competitive forces and shaped by employee expectations during the 1970s, are becoming particularly applicable to an IT workplace.

This chapter explores the proposition that an organizational context that is characterized by high commitment and strong competencies—two of the three key effectiveness ingredients—is favorable for IT implementation. The implications of a favorable organizational context for subsequent phases and the factors that shape it are summarized in Figure 4-1.

Management can improve the organizational context in many ways. It can, for example, eliminate the types of barriers to IT development found in International Metals, Inc. (discussed in Chapter 3)—low technological sophistication, risk aversion, short planning horizons, and a segmented organization that kept IT specialties separate from one another and from the business or-

Figure 4-1.   The Role of Organizational Context in Effective
IT Implementation

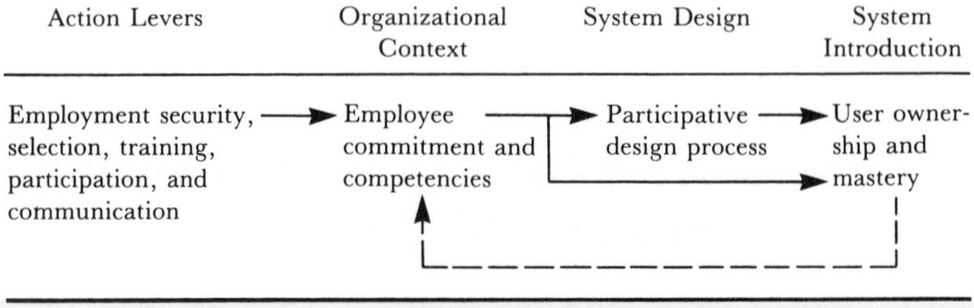

Action Levers	Organizational Context	System Design	System Introduction
Employment security, selection, training, participation, and communication	→ Employee commitment and competencies	→ Participative design process	→ User ownership and mastery

ganization. In the case example that follows, I detail a wide range of factors that helped create a favorable context for IT in one IBM facility. Subsequent discussion revolves around competencies and commitment—first of managers and professionals, then of workers.

IBM RALEIGH, N.C.—PREPARING FOR CONTINUOUS TECHNOLOGICAL CHANGE

IBM is a major user, as well as provider, of IT products. It is also generally regarded by human resource professionals as the American standard setter for developing and implementing effective human resource policies. I use IBM's Raleigh, North Carolina, facility to illustrate many policies and practices that help create an auspicious context for introducing IT.

The Raleigh facility is part of IBM's Communication Products Division (CPD). Called Research Triangle Park (after its location at the center of Duke, North Carolina, and North Carolina State universities) where it was started in 1965, the facility today employs more than 10,000 people. Approximately half of the 2,000 people employed in manufacturing have hands-on jobs in assembly and testing.

CPD has multiple locations for both development work and manufacturing. The Raleigh manufacturing organization has lead responsibility for working with CPD's development centers in product design and for developing new manufacturing processes for its worldwide manufacturing systems. It has also been assigned the lead in training for automation.

Two projects under way when I visited Raleigh in late 1985 indicate the types of manufacturing technology planned for this facility. The first project involved automating assembly and test for a logic unit. Two nearly identical lines, one for black-and-white units, the other for color units, employed fully automated material-handling equipment, nine robotic assembly and test stations, laser engraving of labels, and an integrated information and control system. Begun in the early spring of 1984, the line was operating at near capacity on two shifts in the winter of 1984–1985. Staffing comprised five trained operators supported by several engineers and maintenance personnel. The other project, assembly and test of monitors, was more complex—it involved more robot stations, automated guided vehicles, automated tool changes at many of the stations, and more complicated tests (as for stress, color balance, and so forth).

These projects were an integral part of the competitive manufacturing strategy of this division. During the late 1970s, under threat of Far Eastern competition, division product managers had become increasingly attracted to the idea of sourcing their own products from the Far East, and manufacturing began to rethink its role in the division.

Several aspects of managerial organization at Raleigh increased the likelihood of successful IT use. First, aspiration levels were high. Manufacturing strategy escalated performance standards in manufacturability of designs, inventory levels, quality, and response times. These heightened standards generated a strong interest in advanced technologies that might help meet them.

Second, structural arrangements were in place to facilitate IT development. An "early manufacturing involvement" mechanism, for example, played an important role in the projects mentioned above. Under this arrangement, interdisciplinary teams of manufacturing engineers, logistic specialists, and testing engineers work side by side with product designers to plan new products and processes. A second structural feature was designed to promote technology transfer. Raleigh was responsible for "turnkey" process design. By including representatives from other manufacturing locations on the Raleigh team, management assured the eventual transfer of standardized process technology and implementation methods.

Third, IT projects were undertaken for the explicit purpose of learning. The automation projects mentioned earlier were sequenced so as to provide initial learning on the simpler logic units before workers tackled the more complicated monitors. Moreover, IBM's usual ROI criteria were waived for these projects. Though short-term profit was not likely either from the simple logic unit or from the monitor, the technology was expected to pay off substantially in the long term. It provided, for example, an important basis for learning (1) how to implement the technology, (2) when it might be justified economically, and (3) what were the general implications of the automation process for product design.

A fourth factor that enabled the organization to absorb new technologies was hiring selectivity. Being the employer of choice in the Raleigh area, IBM's selection process, combined with other human resource policies, ensured a very capable work force. Raleigh's problem was not supply of qualified employees, but allocating opportunities to these employees. Management selections for training opportunities and new positions were based solely on considerations of merit.

The fifth factor favorable to new technology in 1985 was a major effort to revitalize the skills of the work force. Before launching a major training initiative, Raleigh managers systematically assessed both current manufacturing skills and the capacity of the existing work force to acquire additional skills. Then they developed training programs to prepare the work force for future work requirements. For example, over 200 assembly employees completed a training program that prepared them for test job openings. Other programs were developed to produce advanced robotic technicians, model makers, and computer system test technicians.

IBM's employment policies were a sixth factor favorable to technological change in the plant. Employment in Raleigh's manufacturing departments had plateaued, following two decades of rapid growth, and recent developments signaled a decline in employment requirements. While CPD projected volume growth at the Raleigh facility, simpler designs and outsourcing of subassemblies had decreased staffing requirements, and the introduction of advanced manufacturing technology would further reduce the number of employees required for assembly, test, material handling, and clerical work.

Despite these circumstances, IBM's practice of "full employment" ensured a positive climate. "Although there are no written guarantees," observed one Raleigh manager,

> we state our desire to provide continued employment for all employees so long as the individual's performance is satisfactory. To provide employment continuity, we will move around work between IBM locations, bring outside work in house, retrain our employees, and relocate people, if necessary.

IBM's full employment practice is supported by a policy of promotion from within. At Raleigh, employees were moving from lower-skilled assembly work to higher-skilled testing jobs, and from manufacturing to programming.

Finally, Raleigh managers also made a dedicated effort to communicate technology plans to employees well in advance of the plans' impact on jobs. Workers were informed, for example, about the reasons for and implications of automation well ahead of the introduction of the logic unit and monitor automation projects. There were face-to-face meetings, including "communication meals," within units, and "cross talks" by superintendents with 10 to 12 people at a time; "skip levels" by project managers; videotapes of the first automated line; and career-oriented discussions between individuals and their supervisors. These communications helped employees prepare for technological change.

To summarize, of the elements that made the IBM Raleigh organizational context conducive to IT implementation, four affected primarily employee commitment and performance motivation:

- *Competitive awareness and aspiration levels.* An understanding of the pressure from Far Eastern manufacturing raised certain performance expectations, which in turn sharpened the appetite for new technological solutions to manufacturing problems.

- *Corporate employment practices.* Relatively strong employment security (but not a guarantee), based on continued good job performance, facilitated employee acceptance of change.
- *Promotion-from-within policy.* Internal mobility, facilitated by
  training, encouraged employee investment in self-development
  as well as commitment to the company.
- *Communication.* Receptivity to technological change was strongly
  enhanced by the strategy of informing employees about the
  planned changes and reasons for them well in advance of implementation.

Another five factors promoted primarily the development and
transfer of knowledge and skills.

- *New structures and procedures.* A number of organizational innovations abetted the integrative design of products and manufacturing processes and the transfer of new processes.
- *Investments in learning.* Corporate ROI criteria were waived for
  projects that promised major learning dividends.
- *Selectivity in hiring.* This policy promoted competence as well as
  self-confidence in the work force.
- *Merit.* The requirement that training and promotions be "earned"
  sharpened the desire for skill-development opportunities.
- *Training initiatives.* The strong priority accorded training generated career optimism and a sense of vitality, and built competence
  to support technological change.

SHAPING MANAGERIAL MOTIVATION, KNOWLEDGE, AND SKILLS

Managers typically are motivated in their work. The crucial
issue of managerial motivation in today's environment is not
whether it is positive, but whether it is sufficiently ambitious to
drive the changes required to compete effectively. During the
1960s and into the 1970s, many American managers in many
industries had become complacent. But more recently top managements began raising standards of performance for their organizations, sometimes dramatically. Higher standards have helped

create a positive climate for IT. The aspiration level of the managerial organization can, for example, influence both the nature of IT systems considered and the amount of organizational innovation that accompanies technical innovation. A National Research Council study of more than a dozen installations of new manufacturing technology concluded that

> the better implementation efforts were accompanied by high performance expectations—major improvements in design for producibility, quality, inventory reduction performances, and so on. Not only are high-performance expectations required to justify the major capital investment, but *unprecedented increments in performance expectations are also psychologically necessary to drive the processes of organizational invention that will help to fully utilize the technology's potential* (emphasis added).[2]

Whether IT is used imaginatively and effectively can be affected by management competencies as well as aspirations. Educational efforts at Xerox and Travelers illustrate the needs and possibilities for upgrading competence of professionals and managers.

Xerox, in cooperation with the Rochester Institute of Technology, developed a one-year reeducation program to help meet the company's growing need for skills critical to an IT environment.[3] Over three years, the program enabled career changes for more than 40 mechanical engineers, chemists, physicists, and other specialists. Computer engineering, electronic engineering, and computer science components imparted new skills and knowledge, including

- understanding of computer and microprocessor concepts and technology;
- specialized knowledge of software operating systems and languages, and knowledge of hardware, such as digital design and hardware interfacing;
- programming experience with at least two different languages; and
- the ability to learn and apply various software languages to the development of microprocessor-controlled products and capabilities, and to contribute to the design, debugging, and documentation of microprocessor-based solutions to engineering problems.[4]

The reduction is supported by funds normally used to relocate, redeploy, or lay off redundant employees. Though modest in scope relative to the large Xerox organization, the program is an expression of the company's concern about the ongoing task of retooling its professional work force for an IT-intensive future.

The Travelers Corporation views state-of-the-art IT as critical to its strategy for providing insurance and financial services.[5] Accordingly, the company is planning a major education program aimed at preparing its managers for an environment in which information will be more widely dispersed, decision making will be delegated to lower levels, services will be delivered and marketed electronically, and managers' concerns will extend from back-office operations all the way to the customer.

Educating managers for the future requires attention not only to their skills but also to their assumptions about human behavior. Chapter 3 emphasized the importance of having a set of organizational ideals to guide technology development. However, official organizational values do not guarantee that the managers who are in charge of a system will manage it in the spirit intended. The managers' personal predispositions will influence their behavior, especially their performance management. A case in point is a study of the Internal Revenue Service's Automated Collection System (ACS), which found that supervisors differed in their use of a computer-aided feature that enabled them to monitor an employee's terminal work and phone interactions with taxpayers.[6] Some supervisors used the capability in ways that developed employees, while others used it in ways that made employees feel controlled and subjugated.

The examples underscore the need for general educational efforts to assure that the appropriate managerial knowledge, skills, and attitudes are in place to support an IT future.

SHAPING WORKER MOTIVATION, KNOWLEDGE, AND SKILLS

One reason for the disparity cited in Chapter 1 between U.S. and Japanese FMS users is that in Japan, shop floor activities had already developed the skills and attitudes required to fully exploit FMS.[7] American managers increasingly recognize that they must develop a more strongly motivated and more highly skilled work force.

Many companies are revising their work force management strategy, from one based on compliance to one based on commitment—to employ a distinction I mentioned earlier. The approach to work force management strongly influences the design of technology, the way it is implemented, and how well it is utilized. Conversely, the design and implementation of new technology can exert a powerful influence on whether an organization tends toward a compliance or commitment orientation.

It is helpful to elaborate on this distinction. The traditional employment relationship assumes no more than employer and employee compliance. Each agrees to comply with certain terms of employment, either prescribed or tacitly understood. Under *mutual compliance* employees are expected to give a fair day's effort for a fair day's pay and management is expected to supervise this bargain in a firm but fair manner.

Mutual commitment goes well beyond the traditional arrangement. The employee becomes committed to the organization and its goals, and this is matched by additional commitment by the employer to the employee's welfare. Employee commitment takes many forms, including initiatives to improve quality, reduce scrap and other waste, and increase productivity. Similarly, an organization's commitment to workers can be expressed in a variety of ways, including strong employment assurances, opportunities to participate in decision making, and programs for training and retraining.

Many organizations continue to rely upon control and compliance techniques that have been perfected over many decades: clear demarcations between planning and executing; narrow and deskilled jobs; individual accountability; standards of minimum performance; close supervision; and general treatment of labor as a variable cost. Though these techniques are often perceived to be depersonalizing and demotivating, such adverse effects may be minimal in practical terms. Moreover, under control conditions, an organization has circumscribed its dependence on the competence and self-motivation of the individual. Many corporations and government agencies still regard mutual compliance as the most practical approach available for managing at least part of their work force.

A few companies have practiced mutual commitment for many decades, but the trend toward relying upon policies that elicit employee commitment instead of imposing control really began in the early 1970s, as management sought to extend to other workers an approach long idealized in relations within the professional work force—challenging work, self-supervision, open communication, and mutual influence. In a mutual commitment context, labor is treated as a resource to be developed, not as a variable cost. Mutual compliance and mutual commitment are not exclusive to nonunionized or unionized companies. Each can be found in both. Mutual commitment is sometimes jointly sponsored by management and union.

The point of this review of contrasting work force management strategies is straightforward—they determine the social dynamics encountered when new technology is introduced.

The Liabilities of Mutual Compliance

Largely unfavorable patterns characterize the introduction of new technology into companies that adhere to a mutual compliance approach to the work force.[8] Managers in such a context tend to be preoccupied with technical and economic criteria, and to deal with social issues only if and when the reactions of employees or unions require action.

In response to, or in anticipation of, employee resistance, management may add a social control consideration (i.e., a preference for a capacity to monitor and control employees) to the other criteria that shape the design of new technology. Management finds itself in the self-reinforcing cycle depicted in the upper half of Figure 4-2. Managements in mutual compliance situations tend to hold pessimistic assumptions about workers' motivations and skills, and these beliefs lead them to develop technologies that, in turn, generate worker apathy or antagonism, which seemingly corroborates management's earlier assumptions and justifies its control strategy.

The dynamics associated with mutual compliance lead to the following patterns of work-technology development.

First, companies design new work technology that tends to deskill, fragment, and routinize jobs. This increases management's control over the work force, but the new jobs also demoralize employees and limit the contribution they can make to service and cost-effectiveness.

Second, the full potential of retraining employees is seldom realized as new technology is designed and implemented. This holds true even though retraining might be advantageous to the company as well as to the employees.

Third, electronic monitoring capabilities built into the work system may ensure minimum performance but discourage workers from providing any more than the minimum.

These system development tendencies serve to limit management's ability to design the optimal integration of technology and organization into an IT system. Moreover, the compliance scenario is also characterized by employee resistance to an installed system. Thus, managements have a strong incentive to move away from relying upon compliance techniques.

Promoting Mutual Commitment

Advanced forms of computer-based work technology are most effectively exploited by commitment organizations. Many forms of advanced information technology not only depend for their effectiveness upon users who are internally motivated, but also can be designed and managed in a way that generates internal motivation. Many forms of advanced IT benefit directly from an operator's understanding of the unit's business, and the technologies can also impart such understanding. Finally, these technologies require continuous learning, and they promote and reinforce it. The self-reinforcing dynamics involving IT development in the commitment organization are portrayed in the lower half of Figure 4-2.

Figure 4-2. Self-Reinforcing Dynamics Involving IT Development in Compliance and Commitment Organizations

	Management Assumptions	IT Development	Employee Responses
The Mutual Compliance Organization	Management assumes that employees tend to be apathetic or antagonistic toward work.	Management develops work technology that deskills, fragments, and routinizes work, and monitors workers.	Employee apathy and antagonism is reinforced.
The Mutual Commitment Organization	Management assumes that, given a chance, employees will want to contribute more and to develop themselves in the work setting.	Management develops work technology that automates routine work and, if possible, upgrades the work that remains.	Employee commitment is reinforced.

How can American managements generate commitment in their offices and factories? Managers are taking steps to share responsibility, power, information, status, and economic ups and downs with workers and their representatives.

Responsibility and power are shared by management through delegating decision making, redesigning jobs, engaging workers in joint problem-solving activities, and providing mechanisms for consultation. Workers are given access to more data about work processes, for which they, in turn, have increased responsibility. Information is also shared through a variety of mechanisms related to business conditions and plans, technology plans, and other actions that affect workers. Status differences are minimized by common parking lots, common cafeterias, and common benefits programs, and by changes in the day-to-day actions of managers which decrease the social distance between levels of the hierarchy. Economic gains are shared by policies under which managerial personnel and workers make comparable sacrifices in terms of layoffs and pay reductions during bad times and enjoy comparable gains during good times.

The policy changes that implement these varied forms of sharing are interdependent, each reinforcing the others. Thus, an action strategy for creating or reinforcing a commitment organization requires multiple changes. This is illustrated in Chapter 6 by a new organization introduced in conjunction with a new computer-integrated manufacturing system.

Two policy areas are especially relevant to commitment: participation and employment security.

Some of the most powerful initiatives for creating a social context favorable to new technology are those which involve employees directly in problem-solving activities designed to improve the work environment and performance. These activities, encouraged under such umbrella concepts as quality of work life, employee involvement, participative management, and quality circles, help employees develop the increased social and cognitive skills and the attitudes of self-confidence and self-reliance needed for the new technology. Positive effects of participation occur when the activities reflect the genuine commitment of management to the spirit of participation, are also sponsored by the union (if one is present), and are accompanied by other supportive changes such as training.

In unionized companies, management initiatives to change union relations usually must occur in parallel with those designed to involve employees. The Common Interest Forum (CIF), initiated in a number of union-management relationships, including those involving UAW with GM and Ford and the CWA with AT&T, is illustrative.

AT&T and CWA agreed in 1983 to institute CIFs in the many separate entities of the Bell System. In practice, the forums have been used to varying degrees. The CIF at Pacific Bell became a major vehicle for jointly addressing employment security issues and expressing a new business partnership between the parties in 1985 and 1986.[9] Local CIFs were established to deal with other matters, including the introduction of technology. A CIF was also the setting for the joint development by AT&T and CWA of training and retraining efforts, finalized in the 1986 collective bargaining agreement as the nonprofit Alliance for Employee Growth and Development. AT&T committed $7 million per year to the Alliance.

Participation can take many forms. The National Research

Council study found that employees are sometimes involved in the decision to select a new technology. At five unionized sites included in the NRC study, either workers or union officials accompanied engineers on trips to vendors and rendered opinions on what equipment to buy. Employees and union representatives were also consulted on how to operate the equipment and organize the work.

When the union is consulted early in the technology development process, it is more likely to become an advocate for the new technology, reassuring union members that the technology will secure more jobs than it threatens if that is the case. Union officials who participate in the selection or preliminary implementation process do this recognizing that they may be taking political risks in order to serve the long-term interests of their members.

Employment security, like participation, is important for its role in promoting employee commitment generally, but, in addition, it is often crucial in determining the attitude of employees and their representatives toward new technology in particular. It should be addressed in policy terms, ideally in advance of any new technology project.

Perhaps no other aspect of the context for implementing new technology is more important than the presence or absence of assurances about employment. The NRC study concluded that "to build and preserve human commitment and skills required to operate advance manufacturing technology, the policies that govern employment security and ease labor dislocations must be as favorable as the competitive circumstances of the enterprise permit."[10]

Many corporations have long provided a high level of employment security. Digital Equipment Corporation, Hewlett-Packard, and Eastman Kodak are well-known examples. Although the policies of these companies were not explicitly rationalized in terms of their relationship to technological change, they have been an asset in introducing change. Severe competitive pressures have forced some companies, such as Kodak, to revise their traditional policies in order to provide more conditional assurances. But other companies have been able to sustain their policies in the face of major work force reductions.

One of the most ambitious American efforts to provide employment guarantees has been sustained by IBM. IBM provides strong employment commitments to its employees and devotes major resources to training, but management has equally strong expectations that employees will move geographically and occupationally to where they are needed and can best contribute.[11]

A union may accept the introduction of labor-saving technology because it helps to secure business and, therefore, some jobs. The alternative to modernization is often the loss of even more jobs. The fact is, though, that the net effect of IT generally is to shrink a company's work force. Consequently, unions frequently make their support for new technology, and especially the organizational changes required to operate it effectively (more flexibility, different selection criteria, and so forth), conditional upon provisions for handling redundancies and retraining programs. Management might agree to reduce the work force by attrition and to retrain and relocate other workers displaced by new technology, in return for which the union might agree to greater management flexibility in reassigning workers.

Upgrading Work Force Skills and Knowledge

In periods of rapid technological change, such as characterizes an IT-intensive workplace, retraining may be the most strategic source of employment stability. Where the technology raises skill demands, increases capital intensity, and renders the system more sensitive to mistakes, effective utilization of manufacturing technology is more dependent than ever on the talent available for operating it.

Rosow and Zager have urged that companies prepare for new technology by institutionalizing "continuous learning."[12] They emphasize learning (the outcome) rather than training (just one input), and show how other activities can promote learning. The essentials of the continuous learning model are outlined below.

- Learning is an everyday part of every job. The line between job performance and learning disappears.
- Employees, in addition to mastering the skills specific to their

immediate tasks, are required to learn the skills of other tasks in their work unit. They are also required to understand the relationship between their work unit and the organization as a whole, and to be familiar with the operation and goals of the business.
- Active, free-form interaction among employees, teams, trainers, and managers is encouraged and institutionalized.
- Employees are required to transmit their job knowledge to, as well as learn from, coworkers.[13]

Summarizing the findings of many case studies sponsored by the Work in America Institute, Rosow and Zager identify several approaches management can take to institutionalize the continuous learning needed to cope with the ever changing nature of competitive challenges and workplace requirements.

1. A number of companies have used a form of "learning by objectives," in which employees participate in assessing their needs and in setting their own learning goals, targets, and timetables. American Hospital Supply, Xerox, and General Electric are among the companies that have used this approach.

2. Other companies have "trained the trainers," developing internal members of the organizations rather than relying ultimately upon outside trainers. This makes the training experience, and hence the learning outcome, an essential part of the fabric of the organization. Companies observed to use this approach included IBM, General Foods, E.F. Hutton, Kelly/Springfield, and Intel.

3. A third mechanism for institutionalizing learning, Continuous Learning Centers, composed of secretaries and other employees who operate similar equipment or are related in other ways, has been demonstrated by Intel. Management initiates, guides, and supports the center; employees participate voluntarily in learning from one another.

4. A fourth way to promote continuous learning is by organizing semiautonomous work teams and paying members for the knowledge they acquire. Teams are held responsible both for performance and for managing their own learning. Within teams, learning is a peer process, informal and continuous. Pay-for-knowledge systems, whereby pay increments are based on mastery of additional modules of work, reinforces the learning process. Among the companies that have used this approach are Digital, Zilog, and FMC Corporation.

TOWARD MORE FAVORABLE
ORGANIZATIONAL CONTEXTS

Many conditions can improve the organizational context for developing IT. Two have been emphasized here—commitment and competence. The policies and practices cited in this chapter influence one or both of these conditions, as Figure 4-3 shows.

A few conditions cited in this chapter are particular to an IT future, such as the reeducation of Xerox professionals, the computer-related skills training at Raleigh IBM, and the mechanism for transferring new manufacturing technology within IBM's Communication Products Division.

Many of the conditions, however, are desirable for many reasons, including IT. For example, most of the Raleigh conditions—

Figure 4-3. Illustrative Policies and Practices That Promote Organizational Competence and Commitment

	Competence	Commitment/ Motivation
Clarifying competitive pressure		√
Setting unprecedentedly high standards		√
Communicating business plans		√
Approving projects for learning purposes	√	√
Using interdisciplinary development teams	√	
Forming cross-location teams for technology transfer	√	
Delegating decision making	√	√
Structuring semiautonomous teams	√	√
Designing latitude into jobs	√	√
Enabling participation in problem solving	√	√
Practicing selectivity in hiring	√	√
Training for IT skills and reeducating professionals	√	√
Engaging in promotion-from-within practices	√	√
Instituting pay-for-knowledge compensation	√	√

competitive awareness, selectivity in hiring, promotion from within, and strong communications—are generally related to organizational effectiveness.

One broad change that improves the context for IT is already developing in many companies in response to competitive pressures and rising social expectations, namely, the transformation of compliance organizations into commitment organizations. The potential of IT, especially IT that informates as well as automates, gives management additional reason to accelerate the general trend toward commitment policies, and in unionized settings, to move toward more cooperative relations. In terms of the theory of implementation advanced in this book, the commitment organization provides a motivational and learning context in which IT systems can be strongly owned and deeply mastered.

Commitment versus compliance policies affect not only how well the IT tools will be utilized, but also what tools management actually develops. In compliance organizations, for example, management tends to deskill and monitor work in ways that perpetuate the need to rely upon compliance techniques. In commitment organizations, the opposite occurs—management tends to find ways to use IT to augment the human contribution and to promote learning. We revisit these opposing management tendencies again in discussing system designs in Chapter 6.

The policies, designs, and techniques for moving toward commitment are increasingly a part of conventional management wisdom, even before they are widely practiced. Though numerous and varied, they have in common the sharing of power, responsibility, information, status, and economic gains and sacrifices.

Finally, two conditions are relevant to some degree to most organization strategies, even those which rely upon compliance rather than commitment. They are employment security and education. Employment security was an asset in IBM's high-commitment facility at Raleigh, and is often a necessary quid pro quo for acceptance of IT by workers in compliance-oriented organizations. We have seen the importance of attention to education or reeducation for a range of workers, from managers at the Travelers to Intel's secretaries. It is especially important to take steps to institutionalize continuous learning.

Chapter 5—Ensuring Broad and Informed Political Support

A member of the Strategic Technology Department at International Metals, Inc. had just expressed disappointment that a key meeting of constituencies for CIM—including engineering, research, management information systems, and business units—had done nothing more than confirm a CIM strategy proposed earlier, and her boss replied,

> Wait a minute, there's a difference between you having made up your mind as a result of having spent four months [working on the issue] and the corporation forming consensus and commitment around [CIM]. . . . The meeting was to develop the common commitments and the working relationships to do something about it.[1]

Developing common commitments and the kinds of relationships that lead to broad and informed support for an IT system helps shape a positive political context for IT development. This chapter explores the factors that affect whether such support is developed. (Later chapters describe how broad and informed support affects development in subsequent phases of system development.) The preconditions and consequences of political support are summarized in Figure 5-1.

With earlier generations of computers, the impact of a new system was confined largely to the department for which it was developed, and top management support was often sufficient. Today's IT systems often affect many activities and multiple organizational units and thus require broader support. Systems with complex technical, economic, and social/political implications usually yield greater benefits for some groups and levy more of the

Figure 5-1.   The Role of the Political Context in Effective
IT Implementation

Action Levers	Political Context	System Design	System Introduction
Sponsor communication and consultation with stakeholders	→ Broad and informed support for system	→ Integrative design and participative process	→ Alignment and user ownership

cost of change on others. Technology choices made in such a context are more likely to be good for the company as a whole and to be accompanied by appropriate organizational changes if all major stakeholder groups are given a chance to assess the IT proposal from their differing perspectives. The more informed the different stakeholders are, the more likely it is that support will be sustained throughout the development and introduction of an IT system.

Few managers or IT professionals would disagree with this premise in theory, but most depart from it in practice. The result: the common pitfalls described in the following memo composed by Rick Herbert, who facilitates system development at Kodak.

1. An information problem is identified by a user group, usually one whose job is highly dependent on this information, e.g., accounting, planning, inventory control.
2. Systems professionals are asked to analyze the problem. In this context "analyze" means to take it apart and study its components.
3. Cost/benefit is estimated. The emphasis is on benefits that can be quantified easily and without controversy. The problem definition and the solution are often distorted to get past this hurdle. Often achieving the benefits requires much more than different information-processing capabilities, but this is not figured in the cost.
4. Specifications are written by a small group of analysts after talking to people they feel can provide the information needed for analysis.

5. The original user group reviews and approves the specifications. It gets management to approve. Management doesn't understand what is in the specifications. Some of the users understand some of the specifications.

6. The bulk of the project resources is poured into the hardware and software needed to implement the specifications. The project is tight on resources. The team members feel their careers are threatened if they don't meet cost and time schedules. New perspectives on the problem are not sought, nor are they welcome if suggested.

7. Implementation consists of selling the system to a lot of people who have had no involvement up till now. Some training takes place, although everyone agrees that there is not enough time and money to do the job right. Other perspectives on the original business problem and new problems created by the new system begin to be surfaced by those not previously involved. This is viewed by implementers as "resistance to change."[2]

This description reflects a sharp separation of roles: users identify the problem, approve the specifications, and obtain upper-management approval; systems specialists analyze the problem and write the specifications on the basis of data elicited from users. The major collaborative aspect of the development cycle is the estimation of system costs and benefits, which tend to be biased in favor of supporting the investment. One result of role separation is that new user perspectives on the problem tend to surface late in the process. Also, because only representatives of direct users are included in the design and earlier stages of the installation process, other stakeholders who will be affected by the system have to be sold on it after the fact. Thus, management's approval or lack of approval is not based on *informed* support.

Herbert's description is a collection of things that can go wrong, not, he hastens to add, a characterization of Kodak's practice. He calls it "a scenario for an organizationally ineffective information system." Later we will review his preferred scenario, "a prescription for better practice."

To clarify the political context of the implementation process I look at four cases. The first two identify the motivational forces as well as dilemmas that limit the development of support for proposed systems. They reflect the spirit of the Herbert scenario. The latter cases illustrate situations in which broad and informed support was generated.

CITIBANK BRAZIL—FAILING TO SEEK INFORMED SUPPORT

A Citibank Brazil database project reported by Schuck and Zuboff[3] and analyzed by Zuboff[4] as Global Bank Brazil provides a dramatic example of the potential costs of failing to develop broad and informed support for IT implementation. The integrated financial database could deliver two types of potential economic benefits. First, it could be used to "automate" many bank processes, leading to better data integrity, increased efficiency, personnel reductions, and tighter security and control. Second, if used to informate the bank, it could be tapped in flexible and imaginative ways to improve decision making and generate innovative products and services.

Both benefits are important to the bank, but project sponsors concluded that product innovation was more important than increased efficiency and control. The bank's new business strategy emphasized the need to develop value-added products and services. Observed one manager:

> Cost-effectiveness is key, but now the opportunity is to make money on technology-based products. You have to have a good automated base to do that . . . but we're now talking about *business* and the role of technology in *business*.[5]

The project manager had a vision of how the system for an integrated database could be used to provide new products and services—how it might increase the diversity of products, the extent to which they could be customized, and the rapidity with which they could be developed.

> Eighty percent of the bank's products can be produced with 150 procedures. The other 20% require at least that many procedures. The database will give us the pieces to assemble in order to create new products.

We don't have products on the shelves in cans. The product is sold conceptually, and delivered physically. I have to develop the product the minute it's sold—immediate materialization of the product.[6]

Though the vision emphasized informating strategic bank processes, development and installation activities centered around traditional automation applications. Early projects, for example, either related to control functions or were viewed by managers as devices for greater efficiency and control. None were perceived to have direct impact on the customers. Consider the following observation of project members.

We went on the safe side. . . . We should have studied the marketing needs. We asked accounting-driven questions, not business-driven questions.

All three areas we targeted focus on reducing processing costs and increasing internal control. What are we doing to support product development? We are still automating—the focus is not on creativity and innovation.[7]

Why this discrepancy between the vision of the sponsors and subsequent behavior? It derived from the project's strategic potential having been neither broadly supported nor widely understood.

The project's two sponsors, the heads of operations and financial control, had explicitly chosen *not* to clarify and seek wide support for the strategic potential for product innovation. Instead, they sold the idea to their colleagues on the bank's Policy Committee on the basis of its benefits for efficiency and control. "Our hopes didn't have to be articulated to sell the project," said one.

I don't know that the Policy Committee would have understood or believed the real business benefits; new product development wasn't discussed. Just keeping the existing factory alive was sufficient to justify the project.[8]

"We sensed there would be enormous consequences of DA [database] administration," elaborated the other sponsor.

But we are low key. We decided to call it "Back-End," not "Data Administration," project. If we used Data Administration, 500 people from all over the bank would be involved and it would never get off the ground.[9]

The sponsors believed that whereas major organizational changes would be needed to utilize the database for value-adding activities, minor organizational changes would suffice to implement the automation possibilities. They foresaw a number of social implications of a system aimed at new product development and other value-adding functions.

- Back-office managers would come into direct contact with customers, a development that would be perceived as threatening by account managers in the marketing department.
- The in-place division between operations, credit, and marketing would become obsolete.
- Performance and other actions would become more visible.
- Many types of data would become widely accessible, raising sticky questions about rules of access.
- Fewer layers of supervision would be needed.
- The job profiles that resulted would give more weight to abstract and analytic skills, to innovativeness, and to teamwork.

The sponsors apparently believed that advancing the product innovation idea would generate maneuvering by individuals and groups concerned about its consequences for their own power, organizational status, and career prospects. Moreover, they doubted that the human implications could be predicted, and were, in any case, discouraged from discussing social issues directly by the machismo of the Citibank culture. Finally, the sponsors subscribed to the theory that, once implemented, the technology itself would reliably indicate the changes required and prompt the appropriate organizational responses.

Because the sponsors chose not to solicit wide and fully informed support for a potentially strategic IT implementation, the project was pursued with an incomplete business vision and without any vision of the organization required to fully utilize the system. Not surprisingly, actual development followed the publicized purposes of efficiency and control rather than the privately held vision of the sponsors.

AEROSPACE COMPANY—FAILING TO SEEK BROAD SUPPORT

Thomas explores how and why the proposals for three IT projects in a major aerospace company—call it Aerospace—were framed the way they were, and the rationale for including only certain groups in the decision processes.[10] His discussion illuminates many of the factors that limit the breadth of support for a specific project, and explains why support is not always well informed. Only when the factors that complicate the implementation process in this way are understood can the support requirement be managed effectively.

One of the projects Thomas investigated was Aerospace's first flexible machining system, a linkup of several machine tools monitored and controlled by a computer and operated by a single individual. The project was jointly sponsored by the R&D group that proposed the concept and the manufacturing manager who wanted the system in his division. For a variety of reasons, the manufacturing manager wanted to "do it quietly." He worried that the union might challenge the proposed FMS on the grounds that it departed from the unspoken rule of one man—one machine. He also worried that the union might try to apply its newly formulated proposals for joint union-management impact assessments for new technology and for company commitment to retraining displaced workers. Finally, the manufacturing manager also wanted to ensure that he was not upstaged by one of his organizational rivals—that he was the "first on the block" with an FMS. Both sponsors concealed or misstated some of the project's economic and organizational implications. Because the initial concept showed a probable payback of four years, against a normal corporate requirement of two years, a variety of assumptions—about projected labor rates, the roles of supervisor and hourly worker, and the account that was to be charged for certain labor—were subsequently revised. In the words of participants, they "finessed the ROI." "We had a number to hit and we hit it," said one. And because it raised difficult organizational issues, the assumption that the capacity of the proposed FMS could be fully utilized by the host organizational unit was never challenged, even though in practice this could be achieved only by redirecting the flow of parts from other organizational units through the FMS.

Although the decision to distort and withhold information helped the sponsors expedite the approval process, it risked incurring problems at a later stage in the process. Failure to address the capacity question, as it turned out, led to underutilization of the FMS.

The sponsors of the other two projects Thomas investigated—a robotic assembly cell and a shop-controllable machine tool—also attempted to proceed quietly to avoid complications arising from aggrieved or potentially aggrieved stakeholders. As with the FMS project, the justification for these projects was framed in terms narrower than the purposes their sponsors actually considered relevant. The necessary approvals were secured, but not without creating border wars, as between the shop initiating the new machine tool and the bureaucracy devoted to servicing numerical control equipment.

When developers and advocates deem it politically expedient to exclude groups whose unwanted influence might slow down or jeopardize the implementation process, they run the risk that organizational concerns will be raised too late in the process and that more complex business purposes may not be considered at all.

GE's DISHWASHER AUTOMATION PROJECT—SECURING STAKEHOLDER SUPPORT

General Electric's successful and widely publicized dishwasher factory-of-the-future made imaginative and sensible use of an array of advanced information technologies. Less well known are the steps that were taken to create stakeholder support, which contributed significantly to the project's eventual success.

The dishwasher CIM was spawned in GE's Louisville, Kentucky, complex in January 1983, four years after conception. During its development, Roger Schipke, group executive of the Major Appliance Business Group (MABG), engineered or stimulated a pattern of changes in the existing dishwasher plant and the other manufacturing facilities in the large Louisville complex. Some of these actions were intended to generate informed support in the management organization for the advanced manufacturing project. For example, to raise their expectations and make them more fully aware of their options, Schipke saw that key individuals from manufacturing, process engineering, and product engineering visited state-of-the-art manufacturing technology in Europe and Japan. In addition, his support for the notion that "quality will be the driver" in the development process gave coherence to the coordinated development of product, process, and people policies in the dishwasher project.

Schipke also concluded that labor relations would have to be drastically improved as a precondition for introduction of the new technology. Labor relations at Louisville had been sour for more than two decades, and the union had on several occasions blocked the introduction of new, labor-saving technology or had undermined its effectiveness after it was installed. Managers knew that the $38 million investment in automation could not succeed unless the union supported it. Management's intention to improve relations and inform the union about the competitive need to increase manufacturing efficiency through labor-saving technology was signaled by a series of quarterly dialogue meetings Schipke initiated with the local president, and by similar meetings held later between the dishwasher plant manager and the shop steward who represented the dishwasher plant employees. Personal relations between union and management officials improved. At a large gathering of employees and community representatives called to celebrate the announcement of the investment in the dishwasher factory-of-the-future, the local union president expressed the union's commitment to the proposed technological change.

The differences between management and us will still be worked on the same as we have in the past, but here today we have no

differences. We should all be scared of the competitors and especially the Japanese, if we enjoy taking home our wages. We should
all want to do our jobs properly so that quality will improve. We all
should realize that plants have to modernize or the Japanese not
only will have the auto industry, but the appliance industry also. . . .
We should all realize that the more modern and better quality
appliances we build will not only keep us the number one appliance
maker, but should increase sales, making our jobs more secure and
probably creating new ones.

The rationale for embracing the proposed CIM was simple: the
new technology might enable GE to increase its current market
share of dishwashers, and each additional percentage point of market share would mean roughly an additional 100 jobs. Evidence of
the degree to which the local union came to support the system,
which was referred to as Project C, is contained in the campaign
literature of the steward in the dishwasher plant. A flyer announcing his intention to run for reelection concluded:

> We have established a Project "C" Committee of Shop Stewards
> and Chief Stewards (meeting each week) to discuss problems that
> come up with Project "C." This way we can stay on top of the
> problems.
>
> With your support and vote on March 15 we will continue the
> representation that you need and deserve in Bldg. #3. *"LET'S
> INVEST IN THE FUTURE."*
>
> *We* are *going* in the *right direction* with *Project "C"* which will
> mean *more jobs* and *job security for all* and the *future* of Bldg. #3 and
> Appliance Park *looks better now* because *you the employees* in Bldg. #3
> *are making Project "C"* a *success.* [emphasis in original]
>
> Fraternally yours,
Don Bennett
Chief Steward Bldg. #3

The traditional labor relations managers at Louisville resisted
many of Schipke's initiatives, apparently because at the time they
believed the initiatives would not succeed. Convinced that they
could not or would not support the changes he sought, Schipke

replaced all of these managers with individuals who were committed to more cooperative relations.

In parallel with its union relations initiatives, management at the GE dishwasher plant sought to build more constructive employee attitudes. The plant manager introduced quality-of-work-life activities and more participative management. To convey management's commitment to pay more attention to the concerns of employees, he sponsored a half-million-dollar cafeteria and restroom renovation. Because the future of the entire major appliance business was in doubt and many claims competed for limited funds, this investment in nonproductive assets was controversial among managers in the Louisville complex. But the quality-of-work-life activities and improvement in physical facilities had their intended effects. A climate was created in which employees cooperated with the introduction of the new manufacturing system. GE management had acted to ensure broad and informed support within the management organization, among employees, and from the union.

EASTMAN KODAK'S WORKSHOP TECHNIQUE—GETTING BROAD SUPPORT, AND MORE

In Chapter 3, we saw Kodak rethinking its systems requirements to align them with business priorities and decentralization. Kodak has also been considering how to organize and manage its information systems function. One innovative aspect of Kodak's approach bears directly on the matter of generating support. I promised earlier to recount an alternative to the scenario for "an organizationally ineffective information system" articulated by Kodak's Rick Herbert. His scenario for ensuring broad and informed support follows.

1. A process is in place for strategic planning for information resources. New problems and opportunities faced by the business are constantly reviewed for possible contributions by information systems technology.

2. When a potential project has been identified by the strategic planning process, it is reviewed by an expanded user set: representatives of all those whose support is needed for successful implementation. Before the project is undertaken, agreement is reached on the problem, the part that improved information will play in its solution, and the relative roles of the users in the development and implementation.

3. Cost/benefit projections are based on the total problem set and total resources needed for solution. Conflicts between local and global priorities are surfaced and resolved. A lot of problems get solved without the use of new computer systems.

4. Traditional analysis is complemented by synthetic reasoning. Impacts of the system on people, processes, and structure are identified, and adjustments are made to all four of these for the best fit. A project plan is created which identifies all of these changes. A user project management structure is put in place to manage the project. Progress reports to user management track progress in all four areas.[11]

To implement steps 2 and 3 of the scenario—identification of the "user set" and expanded "problem set"—Kodak applies a workshop technique developed by Herbert. The optional workshop, which was applied to a dozen projects between 1987 and 1988, has the following elements.

When a project is proposed for dealing with a business problem, a facilitator, such as Herbert, works with the information systems project director and primary client to identify the user set. This includes both direct users and all other stakeholders, that is, groups whose support is needed for the system's success.

The sponsor convenes a workshop of the proposed system's intended users and stakeholders, in which participants are asked to list all elements of the business problem the system is supposed to solve. Participants brainstorm the task, sorting specific problems into four types:

1. Problems that can be solved by a good information system.
2. Problems that need to be solved to make an information system work, including organizational and administrative issues.

3. Other problems that must be solved in order to solve the business problems.
4. Related business problems.

Thus, before the IT system is further defined, members of the user set have agreed on the strategic importance of the business problem it is to resolve; have carefully delineated the way improved information can contribute to the solution of the business problem; and have identified the noninformation system changes that will be entailed. The sponsor then asks participants to develop plans for tackling all of the problems.

This procedure helps generate a problem-centered rather than system-centered project emphasis. Herbert finds potential sponsors increasingly receptive to the workshop idea, which typically improves system design, advances consideration of organizational issues in the development cycle, and generates broad and informed support.

TOWARD BROADER AND MORE INFORMED SUPPORT

What are the consequences of failing to develop broad and informed support for an IT implementation? Citibank Brazil's system failed to address the strategic purposes envisioned by its sponsors. One of the three systems developed by the aerospace firm was underutilized, and we can only speculate about the consequences for the other two.

The cases of Citibank Brazil and Aerospace also clarify some of the reasons sponsors choose *not* to seek broad and informed support. The primary reason in both these cases was to avoid complicating the process, which would delay progress and open the whole course of proceedings to new requests. Seeking broader support would subject the official justification for the project to greater scrutiny. Seeking more informed support would raise organizational issues that sponsors were pessimistic could be addressed; nor were they convinced that these issues needed to be addressed.

Clearly, both costs and benefits accompany efforts to increase consultation in this area, as they do in other areas of organizational decision making or policy making. Sometimes the costs of seeking broader support will outweigh the potential benefits, not only for the sponsors of a project but also for the organization as a whole. Although my analysis was critical of the choices made in the Citibank Brazil and Aerospace cases, I cannot be absolutely certain that the sponsors would have been better off with a more consultative strategy.

Nonetheless, I believe that two factors argue generally for greater attention to the development of broader and more informed support:

- First, the potential benefits of consultation are expanding as IT systems depend for their effectiveness on the support of more groups.
- Second, the potential cost/benefit ratio of consultation can be made more favorable by innovative techniques of the type illustrated by Kodak.

Kodak's workshop technique, which is integrated into the system development process, involves stakeholders as well as users and addresses a larger set of problems. Other efforts, illustrated by the GE's dishwasher CIM, follow more conventional patterns of building broad and informed political support:

- articulation of a broad objective, such as quality in the dishwasher project, to which all stakeholders can subscribe;
- joint participation in educational trips to overseas plants by individuals from different disciplines who must collaborate;
- initiatives targeted at specific stakeholders, such as dialogues with union officials and symbolic acts directed at winning the support of workers; and
- replacement of executives who will not or cannot support the changes required to implement IT, such as resistant labor relations executives, with executives who are committed to cooperation.

These are the means; the ends are better systems.

PART III—PHASE TWO: DESIGNING AN IT SYSTEM

Work to promote the ingredients of effective implementation becomes more operational as the process enters the design phase (see Figure III-1). In Phase One, business objectives, organization ideals, and IT priorities are aligned strategically; in Phase Two they are aligned in a system's design. Employee commitment and competencies relevant to an IT-intensive environment, which are generally upgraded in Phase One, become more specific during the design phase. Design activities, for example, must clarify the required types and amounts of user mastery and strength of user motivation if the proposed system is to be fully utilized.

The chapters in Part III outline and illustrate central design concepts and essential elements of the design process. The theme in this phase is the need for a design that integrates the organizational and technical aspects of systems. System development must be guided by integrative design concepts and it must rely upon integrative design processes. The utility of proposed concepts and process elements are illustrated, and common dilemmas in applying them are identified, through both positive and negative examples. Specifically, Chapter 6 asks what type of design concepts—that is, design principles and design reasoning—should guide the development of IT systems technology and organization, while Chapter 7 discusses the approaches and techniques that can assist in the design process.

Figure III-1. *Phase-by-Phase Development of Key Ingredients for Effective IT Implementation*

Key Ingredients	Phase One Generating the Context for IT	Phase Two Designing an IT System	Phase Three Putting the IT System into Practice
Alignment	Vision aligned with business, organization, and technology strategies ⟶	System design aligned with vision ⟶	Operational use of system aligned with vision
Commitment/ Support/ Ownership	High organizational commitment; stakeholder support for IT ⟶	System designed to tap and promote user ownership ⟶	Users feel strong ownership for system
Competence/ Mastery	General task competence and IT literacy ⟶	System designed to use and promote mastery ⟶	Users mastering the system

Chapter 6—Choosing Design Concepts

Because the paper mill teams were widely dispersed and highly independent, each control room and instrument center was equipped with appropriate indicators to monitor all key variables (irrespective of where they were controlled), which had a major influence on activity within its functional boundary. Thus, cross-instrumentation would permit operators to anticipate characteristics of the product or material being sent to them, as well as the effects of their product on the next unit. Equipment and instruments were grouped to ensure a clear separation between conversion steps, so that team authority and accountability were clear. Manual override capabilities were provided in areas where critical elements of the process had been previously designed to function under automatic control.[1]

These choices about secondary features of papermaking technology—co-locating monitoring devices, giving each team information on upstream and downstream stages of the process, and providing operators with manual override capabilities (open-loop controls)—were intended to support a high-commitment organization.

The mill's conversion process, like ones at other paper mills, was characterized by variability, attributable to the raw materials used in the process and the unreliability of the equipment. Operating equipment involved trial-and-error adjustments, progressively informed by experience and analytic supports. The work force of 240 employees was divided into teams composed of multiskilled operators and maintenance and laboratory workers. Pay was based upon demonstrating increased knowledge of the papermaking tasks. The teams were intended to be relatively self-managing. Thus, the organization and technology were both designed to promote continuous learning and achieve high levels of performance.

In the paper mill, social innovation provided the impetus for technical choices. In other situations, a new technical system will call for new organizational choices. Even simple technical innovations may require revised organizational designs, policies, or practices. Consider, for example, Rank Xerox's experimental spin-off of many of its London office professionals. Systems developers, market researchers, personnel recruiters, and others whose work was information-intensive and did not require close coordination among individuals worked out of their homes as independent contractors, using microcomputers linked to the central mainframes.[2] On the face of it this was a simple change, but a networking organization of this type could be effective only if the company revised a number of human resource policies and practices. For example, in selecting professionals for this new role, managers screened out persons whose social needs would prevent them from feeling comfortable working by themselves or who lacked self-direction. Through experience, they discovered that the supervisors of the networked professionals needed new concepts and skills. In assigning and scheduling work and setting quality standards, supervisors needed to specify and review work *results* rather than work *methods*.

This chapter develops the proposition that an integrative system design, that is, one which embodies the operational integration of the system's business purposes, organizational components, and technology features, is a key contributor to the effectiveness of an implemented system. Figure 6-1 summarizes the influence of design concepts on integrative design and the positive consequences that can flow from it.

To help a company design, for example, a network of home-based professionals or an innovative work system for making paper, we must go beyond our growing understanding of the social impact of computers and the human resource requirements for implementing the use of computers. We must develop concepts to guide the integrative design of IT and organization. The organiza-

Figure 6-1.   The Role of System Design in Effective IT Implementation

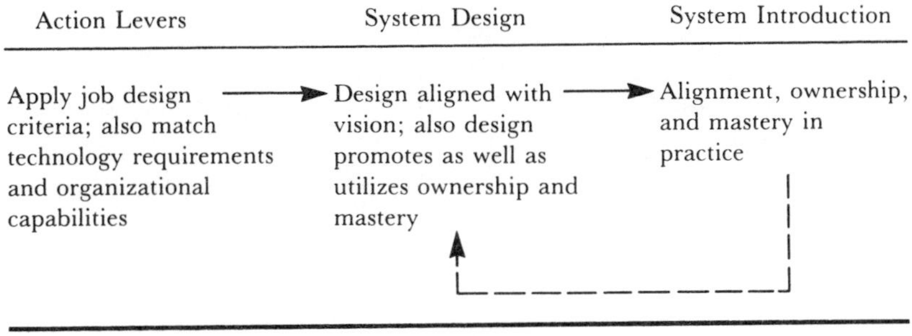

Action Levers	System Design	System Introduction
Apply job design criteria; also match technology requirements and organizational capabilities	Design aligned with vision; also design promotes as well as utilizes ownership and mastery	Alignment, ownership, and mastery in practice

tion must be designed so that it can exploit as fully as possible the potential commercial benefits inherent in the technology. Conversely, the technology needs to be designed to take account of its effect on the motivation and competence of users. Each configuration of technology depends for its effectiveness on some pattern of commitment and competence. The requirements of a technical design can be defeated or ensured by its effects on people. Given these and other interdependencies between technology and organization, an IT system should be viewed as an organization/technical system, and design activities should recognize this fact. Academics and sophisticated practitioners increasingly idealize the IT design process as one of "mutual adaptation," but practice considerably lags the ideal.[3]

Figure 6-2 illustrates a general framework containing the basic factors that enter into an integrated design of the organizational and technological aspects of IT systems. Consider the top three elements. Assume that a strategic vision, such as we called for in the discussion of the strategic triangle, has not only clarified business priorities and organizational values but has also produced a choice of primary technology. (Choice of primary technology refers to a decision to develop, for example, a CIM system for dishwasher manufacturing, an MRPII system for camera manufacturing, an automated medical records system for a hospital, or a network for subcontracting relationships with home-based profes-

Figure 6-2. Factors to Consider in Organization/Technology Design

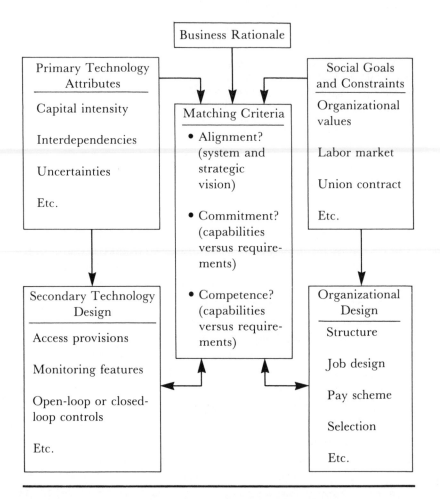

Note: Business Rationale, Social Goals and Constraints, and Primary Technology Attributes are a direct reflection of the strategic triangle vision. Primary Technology Attributes, together with Organizational Design and Secondary Technology Design, comprise the IT system. Following the primary technology choice, design activities focus on designing the organization and secondary technologies, such as access features, operational controls, and so forth.

sionals. Secondary technology consists of access features, monitoring capabilities, and the like.)

In the design reasoning I propose, organizational choices (such as job design) are influenced by social preferences (for example, to provide meaningful work) and social constraints (for example, union jurisdictional boundaries). These choices must respond to the basic requirements of the primary technology (for example, interdependencies within the technology system) and must be coordinated with secondary technology choices (such as whether to use open-loop or closed-loop controls). Secondary technology choices are, of course, also strongly influenced by the requirements of the basic technology.

We now move down to the criteria in the center of the framework in Figure 6-2 for matching primary technology attributes, organizational features, and secondary technology features.

- Alignment—Does the organizational design produce the type of performance given priority in the business rationale for the system? Do the secondary technology features encourage this type of performance?
- Commitment—Does the organization generate the type and amount of commitment or motivation critical to requirements of the primary technology? Do secondary technologies both encourage and utilize the required motivation?
- Competence—Does the organizational design provide the system knowledge, operating skills, and coordinating capabilities critical to the basic requirements of the primary technology? Do secondary technology features both encourage and utilize these competencies?

Three cases illustrate both common design practice and better practice. The case of the Centralized Repair Service Answering Bureau, which we consider first, is an example of common design practice. It is a case of technology driving organizational change, and ignores completely the reasoning just prescribed. The problems associated with this system suggest by negative example the advantages of using *social* criteria when evaluating *technical* proposals.

CENTRALIZED REPAIR SERVICE ANSWERING BUREAU—TECHNOLOGY-DRIVEN CHANGE

One of the Bell System telephone companies began to automate various parts of its repair service in 1980. In Chapter 1, I noted the effects on the testmen in repair bureaus. Automated checking of lines and telecommunications status also affected another set of functions—answering customer complaints, making service commitments, and issuing repair orders.[4] It enabled these activities to be located in a Centralized Repair Service Answering Bureau that served a four-state area.

Customer calls for repair service were previously received by the appropriate local repair bureau, where a repair clerk recorded the details on a form, initiated a manual test of the phone service to locate the trouble, and made a tentative time commitment for completing the repairs. The clerk then passed the completed form to the supervisor of the field repairman. If a customer called the bureau again, the clerk could readily check the status of the repair order. Repair clerks also assisted with filing and other administrative tasks in the bureau.

The automated system received all customer repair requests in one centralized answering center connected by on-line computer to the many local repair bureaus in the region. One hundred answering personnel, called Repair Service Associates (RSAs), manned the answering center over three shifts. RSAs solicited the required information from callers and recorded the details on a visual display console. This information was dispatched automatically via computer to the appropriate repair bureau, which received it in printout form. At the same time, RSAs initiated an automatic test of the customer's service and, following prescribed guidelines, provided the customer with a schedule commitment for the repair. Incoming repair requests and test results received by operators in the repair bureau were passed on to supervisors, who dispatched field personnel to restore or repair subscriber service. Organizationally, the answering centers and repair bureaus reported to company headquarters through different chains of command.

Technically, the new system was capable of reducing both the time required to process repair requests and the number of answering personnel required, but neither of these objectives was being achieved. Nor did the quality of service meet performance objectives. The system was plagued by poor task performance and work dissatisfaction among answering center employees. Symptoms included conflict, turnover, tension, low morale, and the "worst labor relations in the company." Coordination difficulties and conflicts occurred at the interface between the answering center and the repair bureaus. These internal problems led to new sources of customer dissatisfaction.

It required little detective work on my part to determine the causes of the motivation and communication problems. RSAs valued their employment with the phone company, liked their pay, and generally sympathized with their supervisors, whom they regarded as being in a difficult position. Their complaint? They had lousy jobs in an adverse working environment! Interviews with RSAs and their supervisors led to the following conclusions about why RSAs reported feeling "frustrated" and "like robots."

1. Narrow task—RSAs complained about being isolated, physically, organizationally, and informationally, from subsequent steps in the process of satisfying the customers whose complaints they took. They were never informed of the disposition of the complaints they handled, nor did they know the people in the repair bureaus to whom they passed them along. Only those who had worked in a repair bureau had even a general understanding of what was involved in the repair cycle. In contrast, repair clerks in the old system had had much more information about, and had felt more a part of, the total repair cycle.

2. Repetitiveness and constant pacing—the RSAs' job consisted of one short telephone conversation after another for almost the entire day. Despite the varied personalities and moods of the subscribers who called, the job became highly repetitive. The centralized bureau was supposed to promote better utilization of clerical time. Though there were times during the day when the workload was lighter, the load was more constant than it had been for a repair clerk in a service bureau, adding to the monotony and job pressure.

3. Constraints on movement and social interaction—Except for

official breaks and trips to the restroom, RSAs were tied to their desks. They could converse briefly with adjacent neighbors if and when both were free, but the layout limited options for conversational partners.

4. Lack of discretion—Although RSAs exercised individual judgment in eliciting information from customers, their discretion in making schedule commitments was limited, and they were proscribed from giving customers certain information that could be helpful to them. (Only supervisors were permitted to disclose this information.) Many RSAs believed they were afforded too little latitude in supplying information and making commitments. Moreover, they complained that repair bureaus often failed to follow through, creating a sense of futility and powerlessness on the part of the RSAs and engendering negative customer attitudes toward them.

5. Lack of relevant knowledge—Customers were accustomed to dealing with local repair bureaus, and expected the person answering their call to know local place names and landmarks. Because RSAs served a multistate area, they often provided incorrect information regarding the location of the nearest or most convenient phone store. They felt handicapped by their inability to refer to common landmarks.

Most RSAs found their job demotivating, indeed, alienating. This perception is not surprising to anyone who reflects on the nature of the differences between the RSAs' job and the job of the repair clerks. When the nature of each job is described in a classroom setting in exactly the same words used above, students can predict most of the negative reactions I encountered when interviewing RSAs. I suspect that almost everyone who has worked in an organization has formed at least a partial theory about what constitutes a good job and a bad one.

Indeed, when asked to propose a normative theory of the design of jobs that are intrinsically motivating, both MBA and executive education students have proposed frameworks remarkably consistent with those formulated by leading researchers in the field. The model developed by Hackman et al., in Figure 6-3, is the most widely cited in the field, and is consistent with the au-

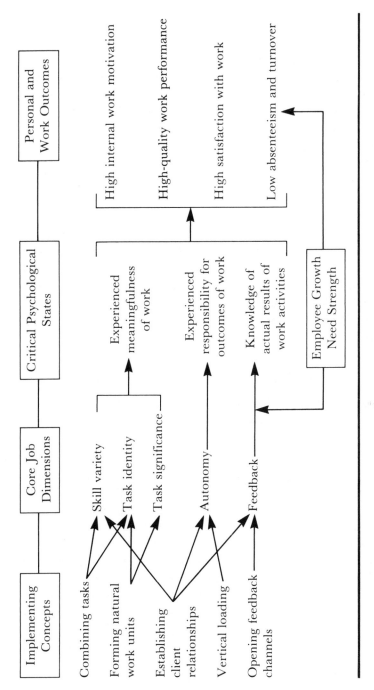

Figure 6-3. Job Design Model of Hackman et al.

Source: Hackman et al., A New Strategy for Job Enrichment." © [1975] by the Regents of the University of California. Reprinted from the *California Management Review*, Vol. XVII, No. 4, 62. By permission of the Regents.

thor's practical experiences in designing high-commitment work organizations.[5]

Hackman's framework identifies core job dimensions—including skill variety, task identity, task significance, autonomy, and feedback—that determine whether job holders find meaning in their work, feel responsible for performance, and have a sense of how well they are doing. How people feel about their jobs, in turn, strongly influences the level of internalized work motivation, job satisfaction, and performance.

Different primary technologies set different limits on the feasible ranges for each core job dimension. For example, it is sometimes, but not always, practicable to form teams responsible for natural work units. This has direct implications for the amount of task identity and task significance that can be designed into an individual job. Similarly, a strong relationship between a job and a client is not always an option for enhancing autonomy and providing feedback. Each technology provides its own unique possibilities for implementing motivational job attributes.

Yet common practice, as we saw in the case of the answering center, leaves little doubt that we have a lot more knowledge about job design than we usually apply when we develop new systems.

Was there any real choice in the types of new jobs that would "fall out" of the automation of line testing and telecommunications? Yes.

Automated testing and telecommunications technology made centralization possible but not inevitable. Thus, the first organizational choice was whether to centralize the answering activity to realize benefits of scale—more flexibility in coping with peaks and valleys of load and specialization of expertise and activity in the answering clerks and supervisors. Focusing on these potential first-order benefits of centralization, the planners neglected the potential second-order psychological consequences of separating the answering task from other tasks in the complaint-repair cycle—the demotivating effects incurred by an absence of feedback about one's work, a lack of understanding of the complete work flow, and the inevitable narrowing of limits on committing repair personnel in a separate organizational unit.

The answering work could have been centralized but designed differently. In rationalizing the answering work in the centralized units, the planners worked from a Tayloristic model of how work should be organized and managed. Again the focus was on potential first-order efficiencies from narrow, repetitive, carefully prescribed tasks complemented by automatic pacing mechanisms and other restrictions. And again the planners neglected potential second-order implications. In practice, the negative reactions of employees threatened to more than offset the gains from economies of scale and rationalization.

Planners might have considered the potential second-order consequences of separating the answering task from other repair activities and rationalizing the answering tasks, and still have followed the same general design strategies, but they might also have explored possibilities for increasing autonomy, feedback, and variety in at least small ways.

The technical/organizational system had been designed by AT&T central staff and adopted and adapted by operating companies. The systems manager in the operating company responsible for the centralized office investigated by the author attended some of the field interviews. He was shaken by what he heard. He had assumed that difficulties in the answering center were the result of deficiencies in supervision. He had not considered that supervisors had been handed an exceedingly difficult situation to manage.

The experience underscored for this systems manager the need for better theory and practice in designing the organizational aspects of new systems. Recall our previous discussion of AT&T's vision in the early 1980s—top management's endorsement of quality-of-work-life improvement activities and a shift in management style. The answering center is but a single example of AT&T management promoting with its right hand a movement toward a commitment organization while it was designing and approving with its lefthand systems that amplified the prevailing compliance orientation.

We turn now to two cases at the other end of the spectrum, where planners designed an organization that ensured the achievement of the levels of motivation and competence required for the technology to be fully utilized.

SHELL'S SARNIA PLANT—IT ADAPTED TO ORGANIZATIONAL PREFERENCES

Conceived by the planning team from the outset as an opportunity to pioneer commitment concepts in Shell Canada, the chemical plant at Sarnia, Ontario, illustrates the recommended design framework and demonstrates how organizational ideals may influence the selection of secondary technologies.[6] Management and union collaborated on, and agreed that the following social principles should guide, the design and operation of the plant.

1. Employees are responsible and trustworthy, capable of working together effectively and making proper decisions related to their spheres of responsibility and work arrangements—if given the necessary authorities, information, and training.
2. Employees should be permitted to contribute and grow to their fullest capability and potential without constraints of artificial barriers, with compensation based on their demonstrated knowledge and skills rather than on tasks being performed at any specific time.
3. To achieve the most effective overall results, it is deemed necessary that a climate exist which will encourage initiative, experimentation, and generation of new ideas, supported by an open and meaningful two-way communication system.[7]

In assessing the special operating requirements for plant organization, the planners identified a need for (1) quick recovery from downtime in order to better utilize the capital-intense facility, (2) control over a conversion process that contained many cause-effect relationships that were still not well understood, and (3) management of a dangerous process involving high pressures and temperatures and semifinished materials that could explode if exposed to the atmosphere.

The organizational design and certain technological features were directly responsive to the three social principles and several operating requirements. The organization of 150 employees was divided into a maintenance craft group, a technical support staff, 2 operations managers, a plant superintendent, and 6 shift teams.

Each shift team was expected to develop the capability to perform all plant operating activities.

The planners revised the systems originally recommended by the company's technical specialists in ways that better fit their organizational preferences and operating requirements. The revisions included

- automation of a bagging operation, in part to minimize tedious and routine work;
- a plan for combining two control rooms to promote communication, reinforce the concept of team responsibility, and utilize the multiple skills of operators; and
- changing rules about access to a process computer to support operator learning and control.

The planners also changed the original specifications for computer control, and developed additional software.

> The necessary computer programs were designed so that operators could use the computer in the mode of evolutionary operations. . . . The computer answers queries put to it by the operating personnel regarding the short-term effects of variables at various control levels, but decisions are made by the operators. Operating personnel are provided with technical calculations and economic data, conventionally only available to technical staff, that support learning and self-regulation. In this manner, operator learning is enhanced. By utilizing the experience of operators thus obtained, computer programs can be updated to further enhance learning and so on interactively.[8]

IT choices at the Sarnia plant eliminated routine work, promoted flexibility and responsibility, and facilitated learning. The planners arrived at their organizational design choices, such as team structure and multiple skilling, and IT choices, such as automating routine work and augmenting operator control, by way of taking account of social principles, critical operating challenges, and basic chemical-processing technologies.

CIM AT ALLEN-BRADLEY—COORDINATED DESIGNS OF IT AND ORGANIZATION

The case of Allen-Bradley, which inaugurated a computer-integrated manufacturing facility in April 1985 to manufacture contactors and relays,[9] illustrates especially well an organizational design tailored to the critical operational requirements of this form of technology. Innovative features of the CIM organization proved effective during the pilot stage, which ended in 1987 when the CIM was handed off from development manufacturing engineering to the regular manufacturing organization.

The strategic vision that prompted and guided the CIM project, called World Contactor One (WCI), was formulated in 1981 when the company, in recognition of growing European and Japanese markets, decided to change its product offerings to meet international as well as U.S. standards. To compete effectively in the international market, Allen-Bradley needed to maintain its quality standards and substantially reduce product costs while widening dramatically the range of product offerings.

Top managers supported the CIM project because they saw its strategic relevance. Union officials agreed to give management carte blanche in designing the CIM work organization during the pilot stage because they wanted to encourage the company to place new technology in established union locations rather than at greenfield sites. Management was required, however, to deal with the union when the system was handed off to manufacturing and came within the scope of the bargaining agreement.

The CIM system translated orders into instructions for each piece of equipment in the product flow. It included an unmanned control room, a plastic molding cell, a contact fabrication cell, 26 assembly machines, and various pieces of automatic-handling equipment. There were 3,500 data collection points for testing and checking, and various production diagnostics were built into the system. Eighty different manufacturing reports were generated.

The system met the strategic expectations. It could produce seven product styles to more than 1,000 different customer specifications in lot sizes of one within 24 hours of order placement, and with zero defects. Through labor savings and inventory reduction, the cost of a typical contactor was reduced by over 35%.

The organization created to operate the CIM was substantially different from the one used elsewhere in the company's manufacturing facilities. The planners emphasize that they developed each element of the new work organization pragmatically, based on their understanding of the requirements of the new technology. Personnel were given broad jobs, and operated as a team. The line was tended by six operators per shift. Each of the line operators had primary responsibility for part of the system, but all covered for one another, and any operator would respond to an alarm in any part of the system. Operators were expected to learn one area and rotate through the other five over a two-year period. Operators also had other responsibilities, including administrative and material-handling duties. The teams met at the beginning of each shift to talk about schedule, quality, and any problems encountered the previous day.

Departing from the traditional pattern, two maintenance personnel were permanently assigned to the CIM unit. Line operators performed minor maintenance, such as replacing drives and clearing jams on the line, and learned from the maintenance employees.

The pay scheme rewarded operators for increasing their mastery. Operators who mastered all six line positions would be among the highest-paid production workers in the plant.

Management was also different. The manager gave operators more leeway in their work and also spent plenty of time on the floor, pitching in on the line when needed. "With John [the manager]," explained one operator,

> we get more freedom. We don't have to report to him every time we walk out the door. He trusts me. He gives us more responsibility and makes us feel like we're accomplishing something.[10]

The selection process, which was extremely rigorous, emphasized self-starting mechanical ability and interest in automation. Training for the initial group was largely on the job. Training, selection procedures, and other policies were expected to undergo some revision as the CIM was transferred to manufacturing and became subject to the union-management agreement.

Although the IT system was not introduced without hitches along the way, the Allen-Bradley pilot demonstrated its productive capacity. But the pilot also confirmed the instrumental value of the organization that operated it. The project planners had generated a high level of commitment, promoted continuous learning, and ensured the necessary level of internal coordination.

CIM TECHNOLOGY AND ORGANIZATION—AN EMERGING DESIGN PARADIGM

The organizational innovations associated with the Allen-Bradley CIM system were remarkably similar to those found in a number of other CIM installations. The National Research Council study referenced earlier found strong tendencies toward broader jobs, team structures, delegation within management, innovative pay schemes, more rigorous selection, and greater investment in training.[11]

Susman and I have proposed a systematic logic for how the organizational design choices found in the NRC study and used by Allen-Bradley (which was not included in the NRC study) are mutually adaptive with CIM technology, and how each aspect of the organization is aligned with the others.[12] The following discussion extends the design reasoning we set forth.

Manufacturing utilizes many different forms of IT—computer-aided manufacturing (for example, robots, flexible machining systems, and automated testing), computer-aided design/computer-aided engineering, materials resources planning, and computer-aided process planning. As more of these different pieces are added and integrated, the appellation "computer-integrated manufacturing system" becomes increasingly appropriate. The more integrated configurations of manufacturing technology have at least five significant characteristics that contrast with conventional manufacturing systems:

- tighter interdependence among parts of the system;
- more immediate and costly consequences of any malfunction;
- output that is more sensitive to variations in human skills, knowledge, and attitudes, and to mental rather than physical effort;
- more dynamism, that is, continual change and development; and
- higher capital investment per employee, and fewer employees responsible for a particular product, part, or process.

The first four aspects of CIM define requirements that call for a certain type and amount of commitment and competence which operators must supply. Figure 6-4 maps these and other factors that influence the design of CIM organizations.

The needed pattern of commitment or motivation and competence constitutes a type of performance specification that must be met by the organization designed to operate the CIM. The cluster of organizational innovations common to many CIM systems—broad and deep jobs, team structures, and so on—make design sense precisely because they can satisfy such a performance specification, in a cost-effective way.

The fifth CIM characteristic—higher capital intensity and fewer employees to produce a part—also influences the selection of these organizational innovations. But whereas the other four requirements make organizational innovations desirable, the fifth requirement increases their feasibility. The smaller absolute size of the work force and the higher ratio of capital to labor costs make it easier for management to afford the cost of upgrading and rewarding knowledge and skills. The smaller size of the work force also makes team-based structures easier to implement. But we are getting ahead of the story.

We turn now to a review of the major organizational innovations (invariably a change from the prevailing pattern) that tended to accompany the CIM cases included in the NRC study, and analyze why each innovation is responsive to one or more of the five characteristics of CIM.

In the discussion of design reasoning that follows, I do not wish

Figure 6-4. Factors that Influence the Design of CIM Organizations

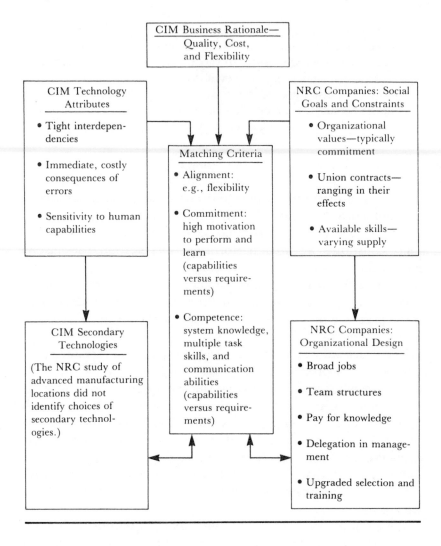

to imply that the CIM characteristics automatically determine certain organizational forms. Rather, I am proposing that the technology systematically shifts the costs and benefits associated with alternative organizational forms. It remains for the planner to actively choose among known organizational options or invent new ones that better meet the requirements inherent in a given technology. Of course, as I have stated repeatedly, the secondary features of a technology can also be adapted to align with organizational realities or promote organizational ideals.

We now proceed through the five organizational innovations that accompany CIM implementation.

1. Broader and deeper jobs—As in the Allen-Bradley case, operators' jobs in the CIM systems in the NRC study tended to embrace a wider range of activities and cover more levels (e.g., doing, diagnosing, planning, and self-supervising). For example, broadening operating jobs to include support activities conserves overhead, while combining interrelated operating tasks reduces waiting time. Both changes also promote a sense of ownership among workers and enhance operational flexibility.

Multiskilled operators in one automated line, for example, had responsibility for material handling, setup, troubleshooting, and off-line repair of defective units—functions once performed by different groups. Operators in a computer products plant had similar duties but were also expected to gradually assume more maintenance responsibilities. Freed-up maintenance technicians, in turn, took on more engineering functions. When companies couldn't create jobs as challenging as these, they rotated lower-skilled CIM tasks and increased worker autonomy.

These trends mesh with CIM for several reasons. Given the tighter interdependence of tasks, flexibility in assignments is extremely advantageous. CIM's capacity for integrating and automating places a higher premium on worker alertness and readiness. With many repetitive activities automated, and the few that remain (e.g., machine loading) performed less often, it is easy for workers to become inattentive. Yet with CIM it's even more vital that workers know how to adjust equipment and when to seek help. Knowing exactly what action to take calls for communication and diagnostic skills in operators, maintenance workers, supervisors, and engineering support personnel. Finally, in view of the high cost and immediate consequences of errors, the time between detecting an error and acting on it should be as short as possible, making it desirable to combine monitoring and operating responsibilities.

With a technology that requires alertness and initiative taking rather than just performance of physical work, it is crucial that operators be motivated internally. Close supervision can compensate to some extent for lack of motivation in technologies that involve repetitive, short-cycle activities, but it cannot replace individual responsibility in the complex environment created by CIM.

2. Work team structures—Allen-Bradley's CIM functioned as a team. The NRC committee found a similar tendency to utilize team structures among the CIM systems it studied. Not only does CIM increase the incentive for managers to install formal team structures; it also makes them easier to implement.

- Interdependence makes it less feasible to hold individuals accountable for a single bounded task; the smaller CIM organizational units, or teams, employed to make an entire product or part can more readily share responsibility for performance.
- Data for diagnosing complex systems can be shared more easily within and across teams.
- A well-run work group is a powerful mechanism for securing commitment to demanding goals, a vital factor given the magnitude of the capital investment involved.

Though most of them relied more on team processes, the companies in the NRC study varied in the formality and autonomy of their teams. In part, these differences reflected the way work groups had operated before the introduction of CIM. In two facilities where management had committed to a team structure prior to the start-up of a CIM, the team structure for the new technology merely reinforced established patterns. The manager of one facility, an engine plant, had divided the shop floor into 20 teams, each with 20 to 30 "technicians." Each team had an individual style of self-management. Almost all had informal leaders, and some rotated the post among members. Some teams met to discuss problems daily, some weekly. All had analyzed and divided their work into modules that workers were expected to master progressively over several years.

Other companies had not employed teams prior to implementing CIM. An axle plant, for example, introduced "shift operation groups," each consisting of as many as 20 hourly employees—12 systems attendants, 4 electricians, and 4 machine repairmen—supported by one maintenance engineer and one quality engineer per shift, plus a factory control administrator. Subteams were responsible for four or five different machine functions. In hiring, management emphasized the development of team processes and sought individuals who exhibited self-management traits.

Not all companies opted for teams. Management in an office equipment plant undergoing a $350 million renovation delegated more authority to operators but assigned equipment individually. The workers, called "owner-operators," monitored their equipment, made corrective adjustments, and performed minor maintenance. But they did not share responsibility for a larger segment of work flow, as they would have under a team system. The company's reluctance to utilize a team structure is explained by a strong management philosophy that emphasized individualism.

3. Delegation in management—Responsibility as well as supervision tended to devolve to workers and teams within CIM management. Most of the plants in the NRC study had reduced management layers and integrated support functions closer to the factory floor. Many had upgraded supervisors, assigning them functions previously performed by second-level managers. In an engine plant with only four management levels, tooling, material stores, and other support services were given to first-level area managers. Similarly, an electronics equipment plant reassigned to first-level managers information services, quality control, and packaging for $10 million "minibusinesses."

This tendency to push operating decisions downward involves complicated dynamics. The GE dishwasher plant's information system, as its manager pointed out, can alert all management levels simultaneously to problems that previously might have languished at lower levels. Similarly, the plant's tightly coupled production system, with only four or five hours of inventory, quickly makes apparent problems that would once have taken weeks to surface. "In one way," observed the plant manager, "I'm more involved in process details, because they bubble up faster and have more serious consequences. On the other hand, I delegate more, because those close to the process have to think and act fast."

Several plants have developed mechanisms for consultative decision making. The superintendent of the axle plant, for example, heads a plant operations committee that shares information with the shift operations groups that report to it. Committee members from finance, manufacturing, engineering, and electronic systems, as well as shift workers and union people, make decisions after consultation with one another and seek consensus.

4. Pay innovations—Innovations in the area of appraisal and pay were common among NRC companies, although they varied more widely than innovations related to job and structural design. Pay schemes were variously modified to reinforce the higher premium placed on continuous learning, acknowledge the increased importance of communication capabilities among coworkers, and recognize the upgraded responsibility and status of personnel operating expensive equipment. Policies regarding pay levels, salary versus hourly status, and the bases for pay progression were also reviewed. Some of the NRC study plants, at least in part to blur status distinctions between management and labor, put workers on weekly salary. (Salary becomes more appropriate as labor becomes a fixed rather than a variable cost, and highly automated plants require the same number of workers whether or not they are running at capacity.)

Several of the study sites replaced standard job classification systems with pay-for-knowledge systems in the spirit of the Allen-Bradley plan for adjusting wages to reflect mastery of work modules, or clusters of tasks. The engine plant whose work teams I described earlier, for example, had 50 modules that employees were expected to learn over a 9- to 15-month period. Some of the modules were in the machining and assembly lines; others were in the tooling areas and material stores. Workers decided, with advice, which modules to learn, and developed plans for getting the training and experience they needed.

Typically, the number of work modules in which a worker can demonstrate proficiency is used as an index of the person's capacity to contribute. Certifying a worker's mastery of a particular module often entails a subjective judgment, however, as does determining whether employees apply their mastery diligently to detect machine malfunctions, perform as problem solvers, and contribute as team members. Whether made by supervisors or fellow team members, such decisions are hard calls.

Piece rates and other pay-for-performance systems that focus on an individual's output are less appropriate with the new integrated technology. Aspects of performance that can be measured objectively, such as throughput, quality, waste, and downtime, seldom can be attributed to one person; they reflect the interdependent contributions of operators, supervisors, and maintenance and other support personnel. The NRC committee did not, however, see any group bonuses, perhaps because few systems had reached the steady-state operating mode that would permit meaningful standards to be set.

Emphasizing team accomplishments does not eliminate the need for assessing individual performance, but it does call for new methods. In plants that make merit adjustments within a pay range, for example, managers have had to change their appraisal system. Executives in the computer products plant reported that they continued to assess performance in terms of individual output for the manual assembly lines but assessed individual performance in more qualitative terms, for example, contribution of ideas and efforts to the group's work.

5. Upgraded selection and training—It follows from the broader scope of responsibility and the critical importance of knowledge and skill that CIM planners will attempt to be more selective and will invest more heavily in training. Future managers will need a broader range of competence than their predecessors. They will have to know the technology and be able to grasp both practically and conceptually the technical, human, and business aspects of production. They will also need to be able to anticipate and orchestrate change in the organization.

In virtually every NRC study plant, management tried to revise and upgrade the way it selected and trained CIM workers. In general, the ability to learn was becoming more important than experience, and some assessment methods that heretofore had been used only for managers (e.g., group problem-solving simulations) were being applied to production workers.

Allen-Bradley's selectivity in filling line operator positions is more typical of nonunionized companies; its union was uncommonly accommodating of management's initial selection of workers. The NRC study found innovative selection processes being negotiated between unions and management despite constraints imposed by the principle of seniority. At an axle plant, for example, a local community college conducted an eight-hour assessment of the technical and interpersonal skills of applicants for skilled jobs. The assessment consisted of a four- to six-hour skill-level inventory, which included simulated problem-solving exercises, and a family night attended by applicants and their spouses to discuss the program. The 45 of 100 initial applicants who stayed with the process were subsequently ranked by seniority. Some declined the new jobs, many because working in the new plant involved shift work or demanded higher performance standards than they were prepared to accept, others because they felt unqualified or were near retirement and didn't want to waste the company's investment. Sixteen were eventually placed.

A unionized diesel engine plant devised a multistep process in which the 250 initial applicants were divided into small groups and given a four-hour briefing on the technology and the duties and expectations of the new job. A committee of two manufacturing supervisors and two union representatives interviewed those who continued. The union reps went out of their way to warn applicants how different the new operation would be, and cautioned them to reflect on their interests and aptitudes. Taking into account the interview results, attendance records, seniority, experience, and evaluation records, the same committee made the final selection. Clearly managements and unions can devise ways to consider criteria other than seniority without sacrificing worker confidence in the fairness of the selection process.

CIM-related training practices at the NRC study sites included much longer lead times for IT implementation, joint sessions for workers and managers, and programs designed to develop basic knowledge, specific skills, and a commitment to continuous training. Management at an auto assembly plant, for example, established a training center months before an automated factory was to become operational and taught its skilled workers to use the new equipment across trade lines. The employees also received training in communication skills to enable them to contribute to weekly problem-solving meetings. Engineers and skilled workers at another plant received vendor's training in maintaining programmable controllers. "A few years ago," remarked one of the company's executives, "we never would have spent money to send production people to courses."

The constant change in manufacturing technology is making continuous training mandatory. Yet even the managers who recognize this new fact of life admit that they and others continue to underestimate the funding and organizational resources needed for training purposes.

TOWARD INTEGRATIVE DESIGNS OF IT SYSTEMS

One of the normative frameworks presented in this chapter is a job design model that is based on a psychological model.[13] Its application to specific situations depends upon the strength of job holders' needs for, say, autonomy, and upon the opportunities and constraints of the task situation. I used the negative example of the answering bureau to suggest the importance of using such criteria in the design of IT systems.

The answering bureau case also provides a ready example of why the technology-driven change strategy, which neglects accepted job design criteria, is so common. IT planners tend to focus on first-order economic benefits and the more obvious first-order organizational requirements of a technology (e.g., new skill requirements and job descriptions). They tend to neglect the kind of second-order consequences illustrated by the reactions of workers in the answering bureau, and by the motivational effects outlined in Hackman's theory. The reason is not a lack of awareness. IT system designers and managers, as suggested earlier, know more about the motivational effects of job design than they bring to bear in the design and approval processes. They tend to continue to be guided by Tayloristic models of work because these models are so deeply embedded in engineering and management thinking. To the extent that they even consider job design criteria as hypotheses, they reflexively assume that the advantages of rationalization and control are greater than the potential positive motivational effects of alternative designs. This is especially true in an adversarial labor relations context. Of course, their assumption is sometimes correct. But it is also sometimes incorrect. It is surprising how often these IT system design tendencies are inadvertently indulged by organizations that otherwise espouse a commitment-type philosophy. Neither developers nor managers appreciate the range of flexibility they have in designing technical solutions to business problems and the human implications of the different designs.

The broader normative design framework shown in Figure 6-2 encompasses economic, technology, and organizational factors. Its application to the CIM organizations observed by the NRC study team is summarized in Figure 6-4. I present this analysis of CIM organizations and influencing factors not to promote a specific organizational design, but rather to outline a general reasoning process for developing integrative organization/technology designs. This process is embodied in the following design principles:

1. Select the primary IT to fit with the three components of the strategic vision.
2. Analyze the primary IT in terms of the competence and motivation required to operate it to the maximum potential.
3. Assess alternative organizational designs in terms of the competence and motivation they probably would provide. Also assess whether they promote the type of performance given priority in the business rationale for the IT system.
4. Assess alternative designs of secondary technology (e.g., narrower or wider access features and closed-loop versus open-loop controls) in terms of their effects on the development of the requisite competence and motivation. Ensure that they facilitate performance called for by the business rationale for the system.

5. Assess alternative organizational designs (e.g., job design and authority relations) against the organizational ideals in the strategic vision.
6. Select the organizational design and secondary technology features that best match the operating requirements of the primary technology and organizational ideals, relying heavily upon competence, motivation, and alignment as the matching criteria.

Although point 1 is invariably the starting point, and point 6 the culmination of the previous steps, the intermediate elements of design analysis can be performed in any sequence and usually should be considered iteratively. The CIM designs in the NRC study sample are consistent with these principles, though the actual reasoning processes are not known. Indeed, in some cases the proposed work organization was initially driven more by organizational philosophy than by basic requirements of CIM, but presumably sooner or later all of the analytic steps were covered.

The Shell Sarnia case strongly emphasizes the influence of organizational philosophy on technology, in particular on secondary technologies. The sequence of steps in its design reasoning process gives more balanced weight to the requirements of the primary technology and organizational philosophy, and shows how choices about secondary technology were influenced by organizational preference.

Social philosophies can influence the design of IT systems, but only to some extent. Consider the possible combinations of social contracts (commitment and compliance) and types of IT (informating and automating) arrayed in the 2 × 2 matrix in Figure 6-5.

The high-commitment organization, which produces internalized motivation and supports continuous learning, provides a hospitable environment for informating systems and is reinforced by them (upper righthand corner). Several cases discussed in this chapter are illustrative. Though the computer-integrated manufacturing system at Allen-Bradley was based on high-level, sophisticated automation of operations previously performed by workers, its net effect was to informate the work of those who tended it. Continuous-process technologies in the paper mill and at the Shell Sarnia plant created similarly information-intensive working

Figure 6-5.   *Organizational Philosophies and Automating and Informating Technologies*

Informating IT	Social contract undermines IT.	IT and social contract are mutually reinforcing.
Automating IT	IT and social contract are mutually reinforcing.	IT undermines social contract.

↑

TYPES OF IT

TYPES OF SOCIAL CONTRACTS OR PHILOSOPHIES ⟶ Mutual Compliance   Mutual Commitment

environments. Moreover, planners in both the paper mill and the chemical plant added technical features that further informated the core work of operators, further reinforcing the high-commitment social contract.

Automating technology that deskills and routinizes core tasks and reinforces a social contract based on mutual compliance is found in the lower lefthand corner. Planners in compliance organizations, as I pointed out in Chapter 4, tend to tilt IT designs toward the deskilling and routinizing end of the spectrum. The automation of the telephone repair answering functions provides an extreme example of these effects on the core tasks of affected jobs.

What happens if basic automation technology required by a business deskills and routinizes the core tasks of workers within a social contract based on mutual commitment? The IT will tend to undermine the mutual commitment philosophy. To offset this tendency, planners are advised to emphasize human resource policies (beyond core job content) that signal respect—for example, participation and self-supervising responsibilities. Whenever it can be justified, planners should add informating dimensions to the technology.

What occurs in the other off-diagonal cell when informating technology is introduced within an organization based on mutual compliance? In this case, the social contract undermines IT, and the organization will fail to generate the internalized motivation required for informating IT. Management therefore must either migrate toward an automating technology or move toward a commitment philosophy.

Although a review of the relevant literature is beyond the purposes of this chapter, it is worth calling attention to the concepts and techniques of sociotechnical design. This design approach, developed and refined on conventional manufacturing technology in the 1960s and 1970s, has been adapted to office settings and to advanced IT. Pava, for example, adapted and applied the approach to both routine and nonroutine office work.[14]

Whatever design concepts are available to planners, designing the most appropriate organization is often complicated by unexamined premises and ideologies. American managers, for example, strongly subscribe to premises about the normality of work occurring *in offices during prescribed hours,* a premise limiting their ability to develop organizational forms and jobs that exploit new networking technology that might better integrate the needs of individuals and organizations. These largely unexamined assumptions limit the use of the organizational option of the home-based professional.[15] Similarly, managers with strong ideological preferences for hierarchical control tend either not to adopt an informating technology/organizational design or to undermine such a design after it is introduced.[16]

Chapter 7—Managing Design Processes

> Everything was great until management took over. It was our system and they got their paws on it. We said fine. You want it? It's yours. You do it. That is when we washed our hands of it.[1]

At issue for this paper machine operator was the ownership of a recently installed decision-support system. The genesis of this destructive struggle between operators and supervisors lay in the determination of who was involved in, and who was excluded from, the design process. The episode is one of several analyzed below.

This chapter sets forth the general proposition that the process used to design a system will influence the extent to which it is supported by the user community and the degree to which its technical and organizational components are aligned. Figure 7-1 summarizes the effects of a strong design process and the actions that strengthen it.

Our consideration of the development process began in Chap-

Figure 7-1. The Role of Design Processes in Effective IT Implementation

Action Levers	System Design	System Introduction
Involve users and experts; give early attention to organizational design and keep process open-ended ⟶	Strong design process ⟶ ↓ Sound design ⟶	Alignment, ownership, and mastery in practice

ter 5, with the discussion of broad and informed support for a proposed system. Here I assume that a project is approved and can proceed with design activities.

Good processes produce integrative designs that contribute to alignment, motivation, and competence. Weak processes yield flawed designs. What are common process weaknesses? What can planners do to avoid them? What dilemmas may they encounter along the way?

Two of the cases treated earlier—the telephone company's centralized answering bureau and Citibank Brazil's database system—illustrate weak processes. Both are near-pure examples of technology-driven change. Neither included an effort to involve all of the major stakeholders; neither project sponsor had a special interest in organizational change or involved organizational specialists; both addressed organizational issues, if at all, only after the introduction of IT produced disappointment.

By contrast, integrative designs are more likely to result when the process taps the expertise and concerns of users, systems experts, organizational consultants, and, sometimes, other stakeholders. Integrative designs rely on direct attention to both organizational and technical design throughout, rather than only late in the system design process. Also, inasmuch as integration is better conceived as a never ending process rather than as a state, integrative designs are promoted by design activity that is open-ended, thus allowing for subsequent redesign.

The telephone company and Citibank Brazil exhibited another similarity: the planners assumed that technology itself had the capacity to elicit the required organization. The designers of the answering bureau system implicitly believed that employees would adapt to the rationalization of work, that they would be willingly compliant. Of course, only if they did adapt could the new technology be effective. The developers at Citibank Brazil kept to themselves a vision of precisely the opposite of compliant employees; they envisioned an increasingly intelligent, initiating, and innovative work force at several organizational levels and in several departments. But like the telephone company designers, they entertained the naive assumption that the existence of the technology would be sufficient to prompt an "appropriate" organizational response.

A sharply contrasting design process was employed for the GE dishwasher system. GE coordinated the design of process and people policies, and the redesign of product and process. Its planners referred from the outset to "three Ps—product, production process, and people," which, though more specific, correspond to the three corners of the strategic triangle.

Consider the integration of product and production process. The dishwasher product was completely redesigned to take into account the capabilities and constraints of an automated production process. The automated process was, in turn, designed in accordance with the new product's features and heightened standards. To promote this kind of integration, component parts of the new dishwasher were designed by teams of product designers and manufacturing process engineers. The heads of the two groups occupied adjacent offices and shared a secretary.

Now consider the integration of production process and people policies. Already conceived in ways that responded to the product requirements, the design of the new production process continued in parallel with the design of the organization that would be responsible for it. The designs interacted with one another; the CIM organization incorporated such desirable features as broad jobs and delegative management, and the desire to reinforce the spirit of the organization influenced some technology choices.

The best example of adapting technology to a prescribed organizational ideal was the dishwasher's final assembly, which needed to remain a manual operation. The line was designed to be "nonsynchronous," which permitted workers to release product to the next operation only after they were sure a quality job had been done. This practice departed from the industry tradition of a moving slot conveyor line, and violated the conventional wisdom of engineering and manufacturing management, which held that the discipline imposed by a moving line is necessary to ensure a fast and steady work pace in this type of manufacturing.

Besides running against the prevailing organizational ideology, the nonsynchronous line, which was proposed after the project budget was approved, required additional funds; hence it was controversial on two counts. Had the idea emerged much later in the process, it would probably not have been incorporated. This particular technological adaptation, and the many organizational accommodations to the technology, were the fruits of parallel and interacting design processes for technology and organization.

Project leadership championed the idea of integrated planning of product, production process, and people policies. The advantages of integrated design were threefold: (1) the design outcome for each element was better for being aligned with the others; (2) overall time from concept to market was shortened considerably; and (3) the joint effort promoted a feeling of shared ownership and reduced incidences of intergroup finger pointing when problems developed in production.

The answering bureau and Citibank cases on the one hand, and the GE case on the other, define a spectrum of design processes. In the next section, we analyze several new cases. The first illustrates in considerably more detail the processes that produce integrative designs. The other two illustrate some of the difficulties and dilemmas that must be managed in the pursuit of integrative designs.

A TRANSACTION SYSTEM AT
ROLLS-ROYCE—TOUCHING ALL THE BASES

We turn to the United Kingdom, to Rolls-Royce Aero Engine's implementation of an on-line system for its purchase invoice department, for an example of a participative design methodology.[2] Managers in the purchase invoice department attributed difficulty in recruiting and retaining clerical personnel to the routine nature of the work. The IT system project took aim at this problem; it targeted both efficiency and job enhancement.

The purchase invoice department checked invoices received from suppliers for accuracy, confirmed that goods had been received, and approved payment. Credit was secured from suppliers for rejected goods. Work was fragmented among four grades of clerks. Each of the approximately 60 clerks handled one or two narrow and repetitive tasks.

After securing top-management approval for the project and for the participative approach to system development, the sponsors established a steering committee composed of senior managers from the user area, a medical officer, and a senior trade union official. A representative of the steering committee explained the project to departmental employees in small groups, assuring them that under a union-management agreement wage rates would not be decreased and that any redundancies created by the new system would be handled by attrition. The committee assembled a design team consisting of the systems manager for accounts, clerical representatives, systems analysts, and the organizational consultant (Enid Mumford). The latter trained team members in sociotechnical analytic techniques and design concepts. The design team gathered data on problems related to efficiency and job satisfaction in the manual system. The team's systems analysts then provided suggestions about how an IT system might contribute to task and social effectiveness.

The team formulated three alternative organizational designs and submitted them to department personnel and the steering committee. The first would create semiautonomous teams, each responsible for all activities associated with a specific group of suppliers, and would replace the existing grade structure with a pay-for-knowledge system. Although this design would enhance work content for most members of the proposed teams, it involved a loss of relative status for higher-grade clerks who, not surprisingly, reacted negatively to it. The second alternative, which would enrich the work of lower-grade clerks within the existing functional division of labor, failed to elicit much favorable response. The third design would assign most personnel to semiautonomous teams responsible for groups of suppliers, where they would become multiskilled, and the remaining personnel to one of two functionally organized groups. One functional group, a lower-grade group, would be responsible for mail and other routine functions; and a second, higher-grade group would perform specialists' tasks. The third alternative was chosen by all of the department clerks at a meeting where the alternatives were discussed, and it was then approved by the steering committee.

The new IT system met its objectives—it enhanced efficiency and job satisfaction and reduced the difficulty of attracting qualified personnel. The rate at which department employees left the company declined, but upgraded purchase invoice personnel continued to leave the department for higher pay in other departments. Subsequently, the department manager was able to slow the internal turnover by obtaining a higher grading for his clerks, more fully compensating them for the increased skill and contribution required by the new organization.

EXPENSE TRACKING SYSTEM AT APC—DESIGN PROCESS INSIGHTS AND OVERSIGHTS

The case of an expense tracking system (ETS) developed by APC Company's mill management to help paper machine operators make operating decisions is instructive because the system's mixed performance can be traced to specific strengths and weaknesses in the system development process. The episode is reported in a case history by Bronsema and Zuboff[3] and analyzed by Zuboff.[4]

ETS was installed on two of the mill's seven machines in March 1983. Eighteen months later, sufficient savings had been generated by some of the 24 operators to justify the initial development. Then savings plateaued. Though one could claim that the system had proved itself technically and economically, the judgment of the developers and some managers was that most of the potential savings were yet to be realized. With regard to this untapped potential, one process engineer offered the following estimates and observations: only 20% of the operators had developed in-depth proficiency with the system, and some of these (for reasons we will explore shortly) seemed to have lost their early motivation; 30% of the operators remained relatively indifferent to the system, and may not have been capable of mastering it; 50% were capable of gradually becoming proficient if properly trained and motivated. Why these shortfalls in motivation and competence?

Champions of the system had decided early that it would be used by machine operators rather than supervisors or staff engineers. Though consistent with a strong company philosophy to delegate decision making to the lowest level where the requisite expertise resided, the idea of developing a decision-support system for *operators* was an unprecedented application of that philosophy, and proved to be controversial. At this mill, as at other APC mills, operators had made operating decisions on the basis of continuous feedback about volume, quality, raw material usage, and other operating parameters. They had *not* had access to cost information. Responsibility for periodically reviewing cost performance data and issuing revised guidelines resided with supervisors.

The project champions had also decided to involve machine operators heavily in the design. Two paper machine operators included as integral members of the design team assisted with the presentation of the system proposal to successive levels of the hierarchy. "I wouldn't allow any managers on the ETS team," observed the staff department manager responsible for the system. "ETS was an operator tool and they're the ones who need to be involved. . . . It was their project, and they made the decisions."[5] "The operators," an engineer elaborated, "helped define cost variables, build the database, and design the screens. They contributed things no one else conceived of. They decided what information they needed and how to display it."[6]

The operators on the design team also bore responsibility for training their peers. Under the plan a first level of training was directed at reducing "computer phobia" and teaching concrete skills; a second level was intended to enhance operator understanding of the relationship among process variables. One of the operator designers explained the purpose of the latter phase.

> You may think you are doing a great job saving money if you're just looking at one piece of the process and not realizing that it is costing you more money on another piece. So you really have to understand these relationships, these interdependencies. You have

to work with them experimentally to see what affects what, under what conditions and how.[7]

This second-level training was never implemented; it was a casualty of organizational difficulties described later.

The introduction of ETS was moderately successful; the strong design role of the two operators contributed to its general receptivity. Whether and how operators used the system was a function of individual operator differences. Some took to the system enthusiastically, and were soon experimenting with it in the spirit of the second phase of the training plan, using the system to learn progressively more about the paper-making process and acting upon their new knowledge to improve cost performance. Other operators, particularly ones who never became confident they could master the system, made much less progress.

Seven months after ETS was installed, things began to turn sour. Operators, including ones who had been using the system effectively, believed that supervisors, who were being congratulated by upper management for the good results, were trying to take it over. Moreover, some supervisors who had returned to the practice of identifying centerlines (operating guidelines) and requiring operators to hold to these parameters prevented or discouraged operators from engaging in the earlier pattern of experimentation and learning. Finally, operators perceived a growing interest on the part of management to use the electronic records of operating adjustments to second-guess them. They began to refer to the system as an "electronic tattletale."

The reaction of the operators was predictable. Many of them began to withdraw. One was quoted in the opening of this chapter. Another concurred in different words: "We were committed to that project blood and guts. But managers want their glory. Why should we support them? They've really discouraged us from participating or experimenting."[8]

Managers offered various reasons for their renewed emphasis on centerlines and for the other actions that restricted system use. Giving cost information to a unionized work force implied more trust and confidence than some thought was realistic. Others observed that some operators, particularly more senior ones, resisted "databased reasoning," and they doubted the ability of the operators as a group to handle the responsibility implied by ETS.

But another dynamic was also present. In yielding to operators the particular function of reviewing and acting on cost data, the supervisors had lost power to their subordinates. ETS was an equalizer. Observed one operator: "ETS is a vehicle for us to talk to our managers. . . . All along we have known the best way to run this process, but we couldn't prove it to them. Now we have a common ground for talking to them."[9] Another observed that "the managers have a bigger security problem than the operators. We have a union; they don't. The company is changing its philosophy. It's a big fear, so they have to be able to show something, what am I contributing?"[10]

The achievements as well as problems that developed with ETS had their genesis in the design process. The strong inclusion of one set of stakeholders—the operators—helps explain ETS's strengths; the exclusion of another group of stakeholders—the supervisors—helps explain the problems that developed.

The heavy involvement of two apparently gifted operators had produced a system that was technically sound and well received by a sufficient number of operators to demonstrate its operational utility. It also showed that it could upgrade operators' comprehension of a production process they had worked with for years or, in some cases, decades.

Leaving supervisors out of the development process diminished the planners' ability to promote *joint* ownership of the ETS, and established the conditions for the subsequent struggle for control between operators and supervisors. Had they been involved, the supervisors probably would have been better prepared not only to support operators who were making excellent use of the system, but also to work with those who had not yet begun to do so.

A second process omission was the absence of systematic organizational planning. The designers made a technical choice to enlarge and support, rather than automate, the machine operators' decisions. The IT thus empowered operators and changed their roles in ways that extended beyond the context of the system. But the technical choice to informate rather than automate was made without consideration of many organizational implications. For example:

- How should the role of supervisors be changed? Are fewer needed?
- How should the style of management be changed to support the new ETS environment?
- How should the criteria for selecting paper machine operators be revised?
- How essential is the type of training proposed for the second phase?

I pointed out earlier that for CIM, an organizational paradigm is emerging that can be used as a point of departure for planning. In contrast, ETS, being applied in a relatively novel way, required an especially active discovery and invention process to integrate technology and organization. Admittedly, many organizational design questions could not be answered until some operating experience was available, but an array of issues could have been identified earlier to ensure that the planning process continued so as to be able to address the issues later.

I now turn to another pioneering system development effort and examine the design process employed to mutually adapt the organization and information technology.

XSEL AT DIGITAL EQUIPMENT CORPORATION—USER INVOLVEMENT DILEMMAS

Digital Equipment Corporation (DEC) employed a user design group in the development of XSEL, an interactive system for guiding and checking configurations of complex computer systems.[11] Users had a hand in shaping the original specifications and reformulating them during development. Leonard-Barton's analysis of this extended implementation process identified a number of principles of effective user involvement.

- User participants in the software development process *should typify their community* in order to represent the attitudes, skills, and orientations that will characterize the system's normal operating environment.
- User participants *should retain their perspective as user* throughout the life of the development cycle in order to perform their function as user representatives.
- User participants *should be especially expert in the task* being automated or informated in order to build the best knowledge into the programs.
- User participants *should develop a sophisticated understanding of the technology* in order to appreciate its strengths and limitations, and should work closely with the expert software developers.[12]

Though each of these principles has face validity and is supported by my own observations, Leonard-Barton's account of this project reveals paradoxes in the list.

Development of XSEL began in 1981, after a similar expert system (XCON) had proved useful to manufacturing specialists responsible for detailing and checking final computer system configurations for production and shipping. Variation in the computer systems offered by DEC was enormous, including, for example, combinations of more than 50 types of central processors and more than 400 core options.

The XSEL design group included individuals who had been involved in the design of XCON as well as prospective XSEL users. After seeing a demonstration of a preliminary version of XSEL, the newly formed user design group agreed upon objectives for guiding the development effort. Back on the job, users in the design group tried out each new feature of the prototype system and fed design ideas back to the XSEL program manager and developers. Codevelopers relied heavily upon electronic communication supplemented by regular face-to-face meetings. The first group of users, recruited by word of mouth, reflected the diversity of the user community. The 20 sales representatives who participated in the original group had a wide range of experience and configuration skills. Over the five-year development, only 4 or 5 senior sales representatives, all of whom were expert in the configuration task, continued to be involved. These active co-developers became knowledgeable about expert systems technology.

Members of the original user group typified the user community, but by definition many were not expert in the task being incorporated in XSEL. Those with less sales and configuration expertise quit the process for many reasons, including the feeling that they would have less to contribute. Efforts to incorporate new, relatively inexperienced sales representatives into active, continuous roles in the group also failed; inhibited by the knowledgeable and vocal regulars, they tended to sit in the back of the room, say little, and drop out. Thus, we have two paradoxes of user involvement.

- It is paradoxical for user participants in the software development process to be expert in the task being automated and also typify their community.
- It is unlikely that user participants who acquire the developer's sophisticated understanding of the technology will retain the perspective of users.

Several consequences of the biased composition of the user design group were discerned by Leonard-Barton. For example, as they came to understand the bounds of expert systems technology, members made few "blue sky" requests. But constructive conflict and tension also declined as a cozy atmosphere developed. Biases also entered into the organizational assumptions that guided XSEL design. Who, for example, would actually interact with the system—sales representatives or their assistants? How would the system be used—to generate configurations or to verify ones already proposed by sales representatives? How much configuration skill did the system presume in the user?

The typical user designer, who was skilled, knowledgeable, and fascinated by the system, provided biased answers to these questions. These designers tended to assume that sales representatives would be direct users when, in fact, some fraction would probably delegate the XSEL task. The presence of these designers also ensured that the system design would meet the needs of highly experienced sales representatives who could construct a configuration from memory and would want merely to verify it. This application also fit the needs of European sales personnel who, incidentally, were less well represented on the original design team. But it was at variance with a trend in the DEC sales force away from its traditional technical skill base toward a more general sales skill.

To compensate for these user group biases, the development team appended a comment facility to XSEL that enabled new users to enter their suggestions into the process.

The XSEL experience neatly shows how "managers can be lulled by the heavy involvement of a few users into the complacent belief that they are in touch with the user community."[13]

My emphasis on dilemmas and sources of bias in the user design group notwithstanding, this case apparently represents a successful development effort, very much due to its user involvement component. Yet, full value of users as codevelopers extends beyond design into the diffusion process, as I will explain in Chapter 9.

TOWARD BETTER DESIGN PROCESSES

The cases related in Chapters 6 and 7 help to underscore the following notions about the strengths and weaknesses of design processes.

1. It is foolhardy to follow a design process which assumes that the technology automatically will elicit the appropriate organizational response, as the Citibank and the answering bureau experiences show.

2. One way to strengthen a process's ability to produce an integrative design is to incorporate organizational as well as technical design activities as early as possible. Developers will produce better designs if they have in mind a systemic conception of organizations that prompts them, for example, to ask early in the process how changes in one set of roles and responsibilities might affect another set. For example, the paper machine operators' increased responsibilities (e.g., for cost), greater latitude for self-supervision, and growing knowledge about papermaking had implica-

tions for the supervisory role which were obvious in practice, and could have been anticipated. Integrated designs are promoted when the processes for designing product, process, and people policies overlap in time and when the committees responsible for these designs overlap in membership. The GE dishwasher experience is illustrative. Timing was especially important in allowing an organizational preference to influence the technical choice about the nonsynchronous line.

3. Involving people with varied perspectives and expertise— users, technical experts, organizational specialists, and perhaps other stakeholders—also facilitates the integrative design. Design team members can variously provide expertise, promote a sense of shared ownership, and confer credibility or authority on the system development effort.[14] The inclusion of paper machine operators and exclusion of their supervisors from the ETS development process made this point. The Rolls-Royce process exemplified an explicit effort to better the design and generate greater support for it.

To realize the advantages of user design groups, management must be sensitive to the dilemmas identified in the XSEL case: users who are sufficiently expert in the task to contribute to design may not typify the user community; and users who gain a sufficiently sophisticated understanding of technology development to contribute effectively to design may lose the perspective of users.

Whether or not user representatives are involved in the design process, planners need to consider how to communicate with the larger user community. Common practice is to hold communication meetings with the eventual users sometime after design work has begun but well before the date when equipment will be moved into place. If the users are unionized, union representatives are often included. In addition to explaining the purposes of the system, how it will work, and when it will be introduced, the meeting organizers may accommodate a thorough airing of user concerns and questions about, for example, the system's probable impact on required skills, jobs, and the working environment.

Meetings that allow for intensive interaction between planners and users, involving, for example, the use of breakout groups to permit more issues to be discussed with greater candor, are usually more effective in preparing the way for the introduction of IT. They are more informative when the system itself can be demonstrated to give users a firsthand feel for it. And, finally, they need to be followed by mechanisms for communicating progress to, and obtaining additional ideas from, users.

The timing of these meetings is a matter of judgment. The earlier they are held, the more respect they signal for users, the more opportunity they allow for plans to be modified on the basis of user input, and the more likely it is that user opinions will be based on fact rather than rumor. However, meetings held early in the development process can place planner credibility at risk to the extent that planners are unable to answer questions raised about schedule, effects on job design, and impacts on staffing levels.

4. A final facilitator of integrative design is open-endedness— allowing for progressive and interactive matching between the technical and organizational components of a system. The more novel a proposed IT system, the more that effective integration of organization and technology requires a process characterized by active discovery and invention. I argued that a design paradigm had emerged for CIM systems which planners could take as a point of departure for developing a specific CIM system, whereas planners for both the ETS decision-support system and the XSEL expert system explored far less charted territory.

PART IV—PHASE THREE: PUTTING THE IT SYSTEM INTO PRACTICE

If a context favorable to IT has been developed in Phase One, and if a system that integrates IT and the organization is designed in Phase Two, then the prospects for an effective operational system are good—but not assured. Even under the most optimistic assumptions about what has been accomplished, work remains to be done in Phase Three in relation to each of the three key ingredients of effective implementation (see Figure IV-1).

Figure IV-1. Phase-by-Phase Development of Key Ingredients for Effective IT Implementation

Key Ingredients	**Phase One** Generating the Context for IT	**Phase Two** Designing an IT System	**Phase Three** Putting the IT System into Practice
Alignment	Vision aligned with business, organization, and technology strategies ⟶	System design aligned with vision ⟶	Operational use of system aligned with vision
Commitment/ Support/ Ownership	High organiza-tional commit-ment; stake-holder support for IT ⟶	System designed to tap and promote user ownership ⟶	Users feel strong owner-ship for the system
Competence/ Mastery	General task competence and IT literacy ⟶	System designed to use and promote mastery ⟶	Users mastering the system

Task 1: Ensuring the IT System's Alignment. When management becomes concerned about installation, the design is usually already in hand, at least to some initial approximation of the proposed system. Presumably, the design reflects choices guided by the strategic vision. Primary and secondary technology choices have been guided by business priorities and coordinated with organizational choices. Alignment of the system with business and organizational objectives should thus be assured. But it is not! Managers must continue to clarify the vision and to assess supervising patterns, training, measurement systems, and other practices for their consistency with the vision.

Task 2: Strengthening User Support and Ownership. Ideally, broad and informed support for the proposed project will have been developed in Phase One, and strengthened in Phase Two by a design that is responsive to the concerns of users and other stakeholders. If so, management must transform support or receptivity into ownership. If support has not been developed, management must be especially resourceful in nurturing it.

Task 3: Developing User Mastery. If the general competence of management and other affected employees was increased in Phase One, a high level of mastery will be easier to achieve when the system becomes operational. Similarly, if the system's design informs and educates users as well as utilizes their current level of knowledge, its introduction should follow a steep learning curve. In any event, the type and degree of mastery eventually achieved is strongly influenced by how introduction and diffusion activities are managed.

The issues involved in putting designs into practice are relevant to a wide range of development processes, from implementing a one-of-a-kind CIM system to providing end-user computing for progressively larger fractions of a company's work force. Consider three generic aspects of the development process: design/redesign; introduce/operate/institutionalize; and evaluate/learn. The extent to which this cycle is iterative can vary. For one system, introduction and operation might occur simultaneously, following design. Evaluation might follow, with no further change. It might also be the case that cycling never ends. Design might be followed by pilot introduction, evaluation, and redesign, which might then be followed by operation, further evaluation, and further redesign, and so on.

Expansions of a system produced by such cycling take varied forms—rising expectations about the system, enhancement of system functionality, and diffusion of the system. System development processes are increasingly viewed in the conceptual spirit of the model in Figure IV-2, which captures both the cyclical or iterative nature of system development and the idea of ever expanding results.

Part III focused on the design element of this cycle. The chapters in Part IV emphasize the other aspects of the development process, acknowledging how intertwined the operating, learning, and redesign processes often are, and should be. Chapter 8 treats the introduction and early operation of complex systems, Chapter 9 the diffusion of end-user computing throughout an organization.

Figure IV-2.   Evolutionary Development Process of an IT System

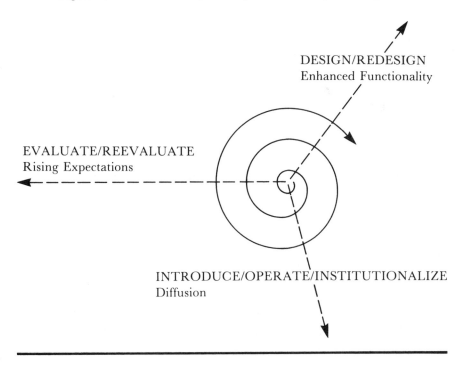

DESIGN/REDESIGN
Enhanced Functionality

EVALUATE/REEVALUATE
Rising Expectations

INTRODUCE/OPERATE/INSTITUTIONALIZE
Diffusion

Chapter 8—Introducing IT Systems

The Kendal system isn't working yet. The people side of it requires much more attention than I thought. The required learning curve was totally underestimated.

The manager responsible for the Kendal unit was referring to an IT system installed a year earlier, a system not yet aligned, owned, or mastered satisfactorily. Some of the factors that must be managed to promote alignment, ownership, and mastery during system introduction are summarized in Figure 8-1.

The case examples in this chapter involve functionally and technically complex systems with many interfaces. The first is a system introduced into one of Thorn EMI's home electronics rental companies for automating certain transactions and assisting individual

Figure 8-1. Role of System Introduction Activities in Effective IT Implementation

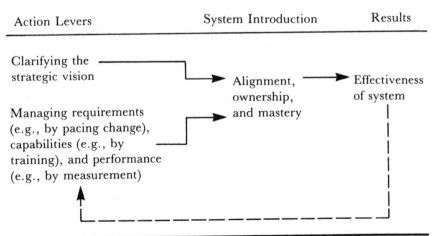

decision making in other areas. The second centers on the installation of the computer-integrated manufacturing system at GE's dishwasher plant.

THE KENDAL PROJECT—MIXED SUCCESS

Chapter 3 related the business, organizational, and technological elements of the strategic vision for THEi, Thorn EMI's home electronics rental business. It recounted the planning and development of IT systems to support service management, order processing, stock control, arrears control, and telesales and marketing functions in the rental shops and their service units. Here I examine the installation of early experimental versions of such systems that relied upon off-the-shelf technology and that were relatively limited in purpose. The Kendal experiment comprised three separate IT systems: an inventory system, a service management system, and remote communication (hand-held units for field service technicians). The systems were installed in the Kendal area of one of THEi's several operating companies, Nationwide Video Rentals (NVR), which sponsored and oversaw the project.[1]

The initial experience at Kendal, which identifies many common pitfalls in the installation phase of new IT systems, yielded mixed results, and the systems' future remained uncertain at the time of writing. The Kendal case underscores the importance of local management clarifying the strategic, organization, and business visions the system should support and checking practice against these visions during system installation and operation. It illustrates practices that can either undermine or support the commitment of different user groups. Finally, it describes factors that can frustrate the acquisition of mastery.

The Kendal area, which comprised eight showrooms and one service center serving some 35,000 customers, was typical of NVR's semirural territories throughout the United Kingdom. Shops, or showrooms, usually located in high foot-traffic areas and staffed by 3 or 4 sales personnel, displayed a range of products available for rent. Historically, repair technicians had been located in the back of each NVR shop, but the trend in recent years was toward progressive consolidation of service activities into larger service centers serving many showrooms. The consolidation of three service centers in Kendal was in line with this trend. The new center housed 9 bench repair technicians, and became home base for 12 installers who delivered rental products and 21 field technicians who repaired products in customers' homes. Several call receptionists handled requests for installation or repair service originated by shop personnel as well as requests for repair service received directly from present customers. A regional manager responsible for sales and service was assisted by managers and supervisors in charge of the showrooms and units within the service center.

Physical consolidation of the service centers occurred in October 1986; the IT systems were introduced in stages throughout the first half of 1987. The systems were initially approved to (1) update stock availability and assist in stock control, and (2) assist with the management of service functions, for example, receiving service requests, assigning field personnel, and analyzing service activities. As the trial progressed, the operating company management added another goal—NVR's operations manager and technical services director and the Kendal system's project manager saw ways the new computer technology could be used to capture customer, service, and installation data that could be used to improve service. The system could support the Kendal regional manager's marketing and selling efforts in a number of ways. It could, for example, make it easier for him to identify customers judged to be at risk of terminating (because of the age of their equipment, service call history, method of management, and so forth) and could facilitate the appropriate action to retain these accounts. The system could automatically prompt other selling activities as well, such as calls to inquire about customer satisfaction and informational calls describing new rental products or deals.

The first two functions, stock availability and service management, were meant to cope with the increased complexity associated with the large service center. The combination of organizational consolidation and new IT system was expected to save time in call reception and field service and management activities. The third function—support for improved service, selling, and marketing—could contribute to the operating company's strategic goal of reversing the steady decline of the subscriber base. The first two functions were emphasized in the initial planning and project approval process; the third was recognized only later in the development process, and added to the goals of the project by regional managers and their superiors.

In addition to the operational objectives of implementing these functions and deriving their commercial benefits, a number of learning objectives were associated with this "R&D experiment." The Kendal experience was expected to generate lessons regarding (1) the feasibility of using IT to manage large, complex centers serving more than 35,000 subscribers; (2) the effectiveness of dispatching field service personnel from their homes in the context of a computer-based work force management system; and (3) the most appropriate organization and managerial methods for an IT environment.

In announcing the IT project to the work force, the Kendal management espoused a high-commitment philosophy. The new system, it said, would "give employees more 'say,' define jobs more broadly, and create an environment that encourages high performance and pride in work and the company." In a meeting with union representatives in September 1986, management outlined the business rationale for the system and potential benefits to staff. Employee benefits included employment security, better jobs, and more voice. Company benefits included cost savings, improved quality of service, and better marketing (by using the computer to identify market segments for local promotions) (see Figure 8-2).

Union and company agreed to "red circle" changes in personnel practices at Kendal, specifying many conditions for the trial, among them:

- the company would experiment with organization, work systems, and roles;
- no current staff member would lose his or her job as a result of the trial;
- the experiment had a two-year life span; and
- no trial activity would be rolled out to the rest of the company until it had been negotiated with the unions.

*Figure 8-2.   Potential Benefits of IT Systems to Kendal Region Staff
Presented to Union, September 1986*

Staff Benefits	*Company Benefits*
Installers	
Better planning of journey sheets	Reduced petrol costs
Emphasis on quality of installation	Improved staff morale
More training	Satisfied customers
Stock complete and all in one place to provide better showroom support	
Job enrichment, satisfaction, and security	
More voice	
Showroom Personnel	
All stock in one place	Less customer aggravation
Stock adoption—can see what to sell and book it	More professional and efficient image
Fewer telephone calls to service center	Ability to exploit local market segments
Higher standards for equipment sent to customers	
In-house training facilities	
Computer identification of market segments for local promotions	
Better relationships with service center	
More voice	

The Kendal IT Project was assessed in late 1987 and early 1988, a year after system start-up.[2] Though the systems were "working" and had proved to be an asset in managing the large service center, they had fallen far short of expectations in helping to manage stock, service commitments, and service personnel. Moreover, their capability for supporting selling and marketing efforts had not yet been utilized, except in a minor way. In addition, the R&D or learning potential lay dormant until the research for this case revived interest in it. Finally, though the ultimate organizational implications of the new systems were still subject to influence, many of the consequences to date were contrary to prescribed organizational philosophy.

Why these results? Why did the systems fall short of expectations? Why were results related almost entirely to efficiency and cost-reduction improvements, with little attention to service and marketing? And why were many of the results at variance with the company's commitment philosophy? The answers to these questions for Kendal are instructive because they identify organizational shortcomings commonly observed in the introduction of IT systems. But before we can examine these answers, we need to become familiar with the work flow under the new Kendal systems.

Work Flow under the IT System

The work flow associated with installation began when a customer placed an order or terminated an account with one of the eight shops. To accept an order, a salesperson checked stock availability on the terminal and removed one unit of inventory. The customer contract was completed, the clerk having entered the name, address, special instructions, and date of installation. These data were then transmitted electronically to printers at the service center, where a data entry operator assigned order numbers. If the equipment was available, it was put in the installation queue.

A "picking list" of orders to be installed was created several times a day. Technicians picked the equipment and put it in bins for installers. This activity was recorded by data entry operators or their supervisors, who also supplied installers' next day's work assignments on a printout at the close of business. Installers who worked within relatively stable geographic areas either came to the service center in the morning to pick up the printout or, if they had already picked up the rental equipment, read the day's installations on their hand terminal unit (called the "MSI"). Installers determined the order of jobs on the basis of experience and geographic familiarity. Travel time, mileage, and analysis codes (e.g., "effective"—call completed successfully, or "ineffective"—customer not home, needs a follow-up call) were entered into the MSI for each job.

Installers might transmit data several times a day, depending on the availability of phones, but most of them came to the service center to transmit over phones located in the cafeteria.

The field-service work flow was triggered when a customer phoned the service center to report a problem. A call receptionist entered the customer's post code into the system, accessed the customer record, and reviewed the service history to see when the last service call was made and whether it was a repeat problem. The call was then passed to a technician according to rules established by the manager. Technicians, who were also home based, received their assignments via telephone. Those who came to the center received a printout of their service calls for the day. Technicians recorded travel time, mileage, and analysis code, and downloaded this data twice a day.

Equipment retrieved by an installer from a customer who terminated, as well as defective equipment brought in by a service technician, went to a bench technician in the workshop for repair and then to the warehouse.

An overview chart of scheduled service calls was automatically created from system data each day and displayed in the call reception area. A bar chart extended on the horizontal axis indicated the number of calls assigned each technician, whose initials occupied the vertical axis. The horizontal lines were color-coded: red indicated that the order had not been picked up; yellow, that the order had been picked up but had not been completed; blue, that the job had been completed. Managers and call receptionists used the overview to spot technicians who were behind schedule or who had time to take an extra service call.

Management Roles and Priorities

Planners had expected that the IT systems would bring about an evolution in the roles, and a shifting in the priorities, of managers. I will review results against expectations in each of a number of areas, and attempt to explain shortfalls where they occurred.

We deal first with mastery. Managers were expected to become more accountable and analytic and to engage in more planning.

Increased accountability was expected to follow naturally from the heightened visibility of the business they managed and the greater accuracy of the performance data. Indeed, the system was having the intended effect. The information system not only provided a window through which managers could see the business, it also provided a window through which the managers could be seen. The following observations were typical.

> Everywhere you turn you can be measured. Before there was no proof of who did and didn't do their job. The system demands discipline of us. In the past, you could wait until tomorrow. You can't wait with this system.

> We all . . . found out how poor we are. The business is so visible now; you can see your performance.

Managers were also expected to become more analytic about the business. Some of the opportunities for analyzing the database to improve operation were cited by the division manager.

> Now we can know the individual's petrol costs, time in customer's house, commercial/technical time ratios, number of calls for remote control delivery, and equipment used. We should be able to optimize the costs of manpower, material, transport, and petrol.

Despite the division manager's enthusiasm, however, these new business insights were not emerging. Said the Kendal regional manager:

> I do spreadsheets and provide guidelines on what to measure. The managers input the information and provide me with the results. They're supposed to analyze it, but they tend to just react to it instead.

Managers had not been taught the analytic skills needed to interpret the data. "It's like giving a man a gun who can't shoot," said one. Managers were humbled by the changes in their roles and by the awareness that they needed new skills. The system tended to amplify their shortcomings. "The manager's role has expanded," explained another manager, "and I get the feeling of inadequacy. Perhaps a more capable manager should be doing my job."

In retrospect, Kendal managers should have given more priority to education. "Managers should be educated earlier," observed one, "not only on the system, but also on managing a large service center. This whole experience makes me wonder if our managers do know how to manage. And it makes me wonder if we get the right people to manage."

The overload that accompanied the rapid succession of changes —the consolidation of the separate service centers, the creation of a new organization to manage it, and the installation of new IT systems that affected almost all aspects of the business—impeded managers' mastery of the new system and fulfillment of their expanded analytic responsibilities. "Too many changes," "too much ambiguity," and "too much pressure" were among the phrases commonly used to describe the start-up of the new systems.

Second, their superiors in the operating company generally expected Kendal managers to use the system in ways that were consistent with the company's new strategy, and to derive general learning from the project. The system could be used to devise better market approaches and promote service excellence. Neither was happening. In fact, the added pressure for efficiency experienced by technicians (which I examine below) was hurting rather than helping service consciousness.

To some extent, this unrealized potential is another symptom of the overload condition, and the lack of analytic and planning activities. But it also derived, in part, from the later recognition of the systems' uses for selling purposes. Finally, normal rewards and measures were somewhat inconsistent with the new business emphasis on service quality. Observed the Kendal regional manager:

> They [managers of the operating company] can't get away from the numbers. They say, "Go for quality," but two months later they say, "You're not meeting budget." And then they turn the wick up.

NVR management had given the Kendal project two sets of objectives: the regular business objectives and the "R&D" objective (i.e., to derive lessons from the experience). Although Kendal management was expected to balance these objectives, in practice, attention was focused almost exclusively on ongoing business matters. Neglect of the learning objective was, once again, the consequence of the overload. The NVR personnel director observed that

> some managers didn't have the skills they needed and were uncertain of their roles. It was all they could do just to try to hold the management together; they were trying to survive. We couldn't experiment with the organization and learn from it.

Performance evaluation criteria also figured in the lack of attention to the organizational experiment. The Kendal regional manager stated that he believed he was being evaluated for commercial success, not for the success of the experiment and the learning that could be generated for the company. "The measurement of success," he said "is commercial activity. So when I get pressure I pull the plug on the R&D part of Kendal and just stick to business." The regional manager's perception of performance measures was confirmed by a superior.

Third, managers were expected to push decisions down the organization and promote employee ownership of the system and commitment to the work. As the subsequent analysis of the roles of call receptionists and field personnel will show, the way the IT system was managed had mixed effects on both employee commitment and sense of ownership.

Call Receptionists

The service facility's call receptionists played a central role in the communication system—one that affected the efficiency, accuracy, and quality of service activities. Consistent with the general organizational philosophy, this role was expected to expand and reinforce employee commitment. In fact, after one year of operation, the IT system was generating two opposing tendencies, one toward a commitment environment, the other toward a compliance environment. This pattern reflected the dual potentialities of information technology, as well as management's ambivalence.

Call receptionists were motivated by the fact that the new work system raised skill requirements and expanded their role. They used the system, for example, to analyze and influence staffing requirements in call reception.

> How many customers put the phone down because we didn't answer? The computer said what was actually happening—the times of day we get the most calls and busy days. We had thought most calls came in on Monday morning, but it was really Tuesday.

Another call receptionist described the increased skill demands in the new environment.

> We need new knowledge: (1) Commercial—we need to know products well enough to talk to the customer. For example, we have to recognize how old the set is. If they've had it for five years we should ask if they're interested in changing. (2) Service—we need to know enough to talk to customers about their problems. (3) Installation queries—we have to know about this part of the business, too, because people will call us about new service.

As an example of role expansion, responsibility for creating the daily allocation table for field technician assignments was assumed by a call receptionist, the manager only approving the finished table. The regional manager intended to further expand the call receptionist's role to include telesales.

Demotivating effects on call receptionists, deriving from the pacing and monitoring features of the system, were incipient. The system automatically gave receptionists a six-second delay after each call "to complete the request after the customer hangs up," but it also recorded how they spent their time. For each receptionist it calculated the number of calls during any specified time period, the times logged on and off (e.g., at beginning of day, for lunch, breaks, at end of day), and "time suspended" (i.e., the time the receptionist turned her phone off and did not accept any calls because she was doing something else). Seeing printouts showing how they spent their time, receptionists complained that "you can't tell from the printout what we're actually doing on the phone with the customer." In anticipation of management inquiry, several receptionists kept diaries. "I manually write down what I'm doing during the busy times," explained one.

> The printout is just one explanation of why we may have more abandoned calls during a certain time period. I want to be able to remember why we weren't able to answer all the calls.

If concerns about fairness and the tendency to develop defensive records in reaction to detailed performance measurement increased, it would undermine the call receptionists' generally positive response to their work. This trend would continue if their supervisor failed to recognize the potentially self-defeating consequence of measurement and did not act to reduce their concerns and defensiveness. In fact, management had not yet perceived and addressed the dual potentialities of the IT system when the study was conducted.

Installers and Field Technicians

The operating company's business strategy called for installers and field repair technicians to become more sales oriented. These field personnel had direct contact with customers in their homes, and could shape the customer's image of the company by their courtesy and competence. They could make sales on the spot by promoting new products or suggesting an upgrade to the customer's existing rental equipment. Finally, they could gather information about the customer (such as the size of the household and the nature of other appliances) that might be useful in identifying subscribers for targeted promotional campaigns. Hopefully, the IT system could be managed in a way that encouraged such role development.

Recall that the company's stated organization strategy called for employees, including field personnel, to have "more say" and "more broadly defined jobs," and to work in "an environment that encourages high performance." Against these expectations, results were mixed but mostly disappointing. Regarding business priorities, the system's effect on the customer and sales orientation of field technicians was the opposite of strategic requirements. Regarding organizational implications, the new system was experienced by a few technicians as positive in certain respects but was generally a turn-off because of its heavy control orientation. Field personnel's few positive remarks about the new system applauded the time it saved and the amount of customer information it enabled them to review before a call.

Field personnel's limited mastery of the system was due largely to the extremely limited instruction and training they received. According to the office manager,

> Technicians weren't really told the purpose of the system—"Why are we doing this?" In the back of their minds some are afraid. "If I'm more efficient they'll need fewer of us."

Everyone seemed to need a better understanding of the work flows and the importance of their work in an interdependent system.

> With one error in a customer address, a technician goes to the wrong house. That means he'll probably miss the three calls at the end of the day. Three customers are frustrated and each makes three calls to the showroom.

Many of the field personnel felt depersonalized by the computer-mediated communication. They also felt lonely because of the arrangement of working out of their homes and communicating by phone and MSI.

Even more important in undermining worker commitment were the monitoring and measurement of performance. Workers were given "effectiveness ratings" generated by the IT system. Printouts listed for each technician the number of days worked, number of effective and ineffective calls, average cost of a service call, and "grade of service" (i.e., percentage of effective calls).

Effectiveness-rating printouts for installers, highlighting the lowest and highest performers, were posted on a notice board in the warehouse. Technicians' performance data, like those of their managers, were more visible and less readily manipulated in the new system. Workers were concerned that effectiveness ratings, while technically accurate, provided an incomplete picture of performance. One installer explained that

> a noneffective call is not a personal error! The person may not have been at home. And we're just one link at the end of a chain. Errors that occur in the shop or workroom only show up in installation. The measurement is too final and only points to one link in the chain.

One manager said that he had not yet used the information as a stick; he used it to "pull workers aside and give them an informal reprimand." A technician had a different perspective. "They ask you, 'What did you do during those two hours?' It's draining to answer all their bloody questions."

Many technicians referred to MSI as an acronym for a spy network. "It's a spy in the camp," said one; "it knows exactly what you do." A field technician admitted that he kept a manual diary of his activities as protection against management inquiries. "I've started to write a diary of what I do every hour. That way when they ask I'll be able to defend myself."

The pressure to meet quantitative performance measures led many technicians and installers to put customer satisfaction second. One installer explained, "There's so much pressure from the company to meet the numbers, most technicians don't put forth the effort to give a demo. They wipe the sweat from their brow if they just get it tuned and the customer signs."

In general, computer-generated information on performance was used by superiors to manage subordinates; it was not used by individuals for self-management. One worker summed up the situation thus:

> They call it "management information systems"; the perception is that it's just for managers. The cost/job/day information goes to the managers. Usually they do not give that information to workers. They should, the data speaks for itself. Managers say by their actions, "I am a manager and I measure your performance." They

should say, "I trust you and the information; you're an adult, you do something with it."

Finally, the system was expected to free up managers' time, enabling them to get into the field with the technicians and installation workers they supervised. This had not happened. Instead, managers were "glued to their chairs." Some managers referred to themselves as "slaves to the system." One explanation was that the system had not stabilized to the point where managers felt they could leave the office. Another held that "with these systems it's too easy to manage from a sedentary position." Managers could sit at their terminals and "see exactly what is happening in the service center organization."

Digging Deeper to Diagnose the Kendal Project

The preceding might be called a first-level explanation for the disappointing outcomes at Kendal after one year. It attributes the shortcomings in alignment, ownership, and mastery of the system to the following factors:

- too little training and knowledge;
- failure to provide additional resources during start-up, resulting in severe overload;
- identification of a role for system support of selling and marketing only after initial planning had emphasized efficiency functions;
- rewards that emphasized operational efficiency;
- heavy use of the IT system to monitor quantitative aspects of behavior and performance; and
- overreliance on the system for remote communication.

These factors raise the general question of "Why?" Why, for example, too little training? Why the failure to adjust the reward system? And so on (see Figure 8-3).

Kendal managers underestimated the requirements for additional resources, management attention, and training because they focused almost exclusively on the technical system. Although discussion of commercial objectives also referred to marketing and

Figure 8-3. **Diagnosis of Kendal Project after One Year**

Underlying Explanations	First-Level Explanations for Results	Mostly Disappointing Results
	Affecting Managers	**Slow Development of Managers' Mastery**
	Visibility, accuracy of data (+)	More accounta-
	Too little education and training	bility, but slow development of analytic skill and knowledge of
Neglected to align IT to the vision; underestimated effort needed to manage organiza- tional aspects of IT system; failed to see role of HR experts, consul- tants, and user involvement	Overload from pace of change	the business
	Quantitative bias of measurements	**System Misaligned with Business Priorities**
	Efficiency bias of rewards	Managers fail to use customer data-
	Lack of staff	base for marketing, and undermine rather than upgrade service emphasis
Did not understand dual potentialities of IT, e.g., for self-management versus closer supervision, and for freeing up supervisors to spend time with field personnel versus promoting remote control of them	**Affecting Call Receptionists**	Managers fail to balance ongoing business and learning objec- tives during pilot
	Expanded role and knowledge (+)	
	Monitoring and measurements	
	Affecting Field Personnel	**System Failing to Elicit Strong Ownership**
	Time saved (+)	Call receptionists motivated by job
	Additional perspective on business (+)	but defensive about performance monitoring
	Monitoring and measuring quantity, not quality of work; posting of performance rankings	Field personnel responses primarily negative, e.g.,
	Remote debriefing	depersonalized, lonely, defensive

growth, in the end managers did what they were in the habit of doing—they emphasized control and efficiency. Similarly, though managers did articulate organizational objectives, their commitment to them was weak. According to one higher-level manager: "They just did not think that organizational issues were that important . . . they perceived that they would get the best out of the system with authoritarian management."

In brief, Kendal managers had not clarified a vision for the local project that aligned with the company's organizational and business priorities, partly because these priorities were only recently formulated by the operating company in response to THEi's strategic vision.

In addition, Kendal managers underestimated the magnitude of the human resources task. Said the regional manager: "Nobody knew what Kendal could and couldn't do; it's evolving. It's like entering a tunnel and not knowing where you are going."

One reason for underestimating the size of this task was the implicit assumption that technology will drive the necessary change. An external consultant was asked by higher management to visit the facility during the start-up period. "Our visit," he observed, "showed that the development has . . . been primarily technology-driven. The impact on and of the people involved has had less significant consideration. This is . . . understandable, given the *speed* at which the changes have been driven."

Kendal managers had declined a suggestion by NVR executives that they involve organizational consultants and/or the company's human resource specialists in the planning and implementation of the system. Their strong emphasis on the technology had led them to exclude specialists who might have helped them learn from the experience and who might have directed their attention to the people aspects of the system.

Chapter 3 reported that the CEO of THEi decided to educate his top management team about the strategic relationships among business, organization, and IT strategies. When he authorized the case study of Kendal to be developed as an educational vehicle for this top management group, he set in motion a process by which other regions of NVR began to tap Kendal's experience, and the Kendal region undertook to address the problems reported here.

The Kendal case underscores the need for management to ensure that an installed system is consistent with business priorities and organizational philosophy, in other words, to align the strategic triangle in action. Many dynamics can make this difficult, including tendencies to let technology drive change and old organizational habits that prevail even when they are at variance with the vision. In the Kendal case, we also see how user ownership of the IT system was limited both by management's control-oriented interpretation of its capabilities and by the minimal involvement of the field force in the planning and introduction of the system.

Although the Kendal case contains lessons in all three tasks—managing alignment, managing ownership, and managing mastery—our analysis emphasized only the first two. While the slow development of mastery was also a major factor in the Kendal system's shortfalls, the importance of managing for learning and mastery is revealed more clearly in the problems encountered during the start-up of GE's CIM system for producing dishwashers.

GE'S DISHWASHER CIM START-UP—SUCCESS IN DEVELOPING MASTERY

The GE dishwasher CIM, as we observed earlier, was a highly successful project, with spectacular commercial results. The broad and informed support generated early in the development process by actions described in Chapter 5 was sustained during installation, and although temporary compromises were made in the concept of continuous flow when project managers deemed it necessary to add buffer inventories, the project generally tracked well with the strategic vision during start-up. The most instructive facet of the dishwasher start-up was the challenge to management to develop adequate mastery.

Requirements and Capabilities Curves

Start-ups of new technologies can be characterized by two curves—a requirement curve and a capability curve—that combine to create what I call the "bow tie" dilemma (see Figure 8-4).

Figure 8-4. Bow Tie Dilemma of Fixed Automation

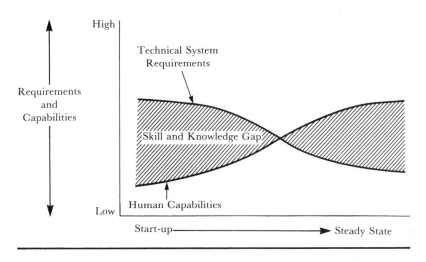

The first curve traces the level of expertise required by the technology from start-up to steady state and beyond. For example, when CIM technology is first installed, relatively high levels of technical expertise and group problem-solving capabilities are needed to learn its operating characteristics, synchronize its various parts, and debug it. As a system is brought on-line and fine-tuned, less expertise is required to operate and maintain it. Hence, the downward-sloping requirements curve.

The second curve traces the normal development of relevant human capabilities, which are relatively low at the time of installation and grow throughout the start-up period, tending to level off at some point if and when the system reaches a steady state.

The two curves normally define a knowledge and skill *deficit* in early phases of the start-up and (assuming for the moment stable application of the technology) an emerging *surplus* of capabilities over time.

The precise shape of each of these curves and the crossover point from skill gap to skill surplus (if it actually occurs) depend upon the nature of the new technology (how readily it can be routinized) and the human system (how much it promotes learning).

A skill surplus may not materialize if certain conditions exist.

For example, the technology may continue to be enhanced, modified, or applied in new ways, creating a succession of requirement
curves. Before a version of the technology becomes sufficiently
routinized that the requirements bottom out, the system is elaborated or modified to create a new requirement curve. This dynamic by itself tends to continually postpone the development of
surplus operating skill and knowledge. A similar succession of
mastery curves can result from personnel turnover, also tending to
postpone the surplus (see Figure 8-5). In addition, the curves are
related to one another; each modification or new application of the
technology can trigger new learning.

Requirements of the Dishwasher Project Start-Up

The GE dishwasher case illustrates how early requirements of
the technology and capabilities of the organization create a skill

*Figure 8-5. Technical System Requirements and Human Capabilities
with Continually Developing IT System*

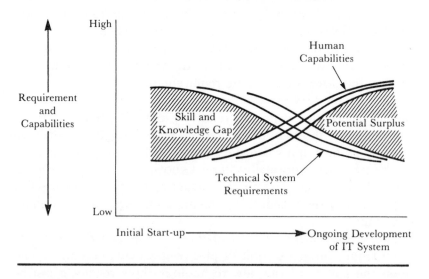

Note: System evolution creates a never ending series of technical system requirements curves to take advantage of developing human capabilities. This evolution
also creates a never ending series of human capabilities curves. In combination,
the successions of curves postpone the skill surplus.

gap, and analyzes some techniques that can be used to close the gap. Competent management of the dishwasher project start-up was not only a technical and commercial objective, but also a political necessity, according to the plant manager.

> It took us two months to get running smoothly—we sweated out these two months. For the first nine weeks we got out the planned volume through dedicated joint efforts by the project group and the production operation. This was a period of great suspense for us. We in MABG [Major Appliance Business Group] had a long history that we could not implement a project on time, we wasted people, and we got half of the business promised. The corporation was making other divestitures. We believed that we could be sold by GE, especially if there was evidence that the group was not managing this project effectively. Managers in the group's other businesses were commenting to the effect that this project would be no different.

A description of the new system will help to convey the ambitiousness of the change from conventional to automated manufacturing. The new CIM mechanically links seven islands of automation with a 2.9 mile, power-and-free conveyor transfer and storage system that replaces about nine miles of conventional monorail conveyor. The more than 10,000 tub and door carriers previously needed on the conveyors were reduced to 800 when the project was fully implemented. Previously, the tubs and doors were manually handled 27 times as they made their five-day cycle through the plant. In the new system, the doors are handled only three times and the tub only once. According to plan, a dishwasher travels through the manufacturing process and to the warehouse in less than a day. Many of the fabricated parts are made right next to the assembly station where the part is needed. The factory has a total of 24 programmable controllers with extensive data-processing capabilities and five CRT terminals. Test and repair data flow, real time, into the plant quality information system, where they can be accessed by quality control engineers and shop operations managers. This immediate feedback allows rapid trend analysis, root cause determination, and corrective actions.

Given the radical changes precipitated by the CIM, the technical uncertainty of the system would inevitably be initially high and pertinent capabilities relative low.

The following events and circumstances further illustrate the very demanding requirements of start-up. During pilot runs, the power-and-free conveyor system was plagued with both hardware and software problems and the material-handling equipment in the test area didn't work. The quality of parts produced by older equipment within the larger dishwasher facility did not meet the more demanding tolerances required by the automated equipment. With the tightly coupled nature of the system, even small problems in any of a number of areas quickly generated compounded effects in other areas. Exacerbating these technical challenges was an unplanned increase in demand for the new product.

Capabilities in the Start-Up

Making implementation more challenging still, several factors slowed accumulation of the requisite skills and knowledge. Management had been unable to negotiate a change in the traditional way ability and seniority were balanced. Managers classified the new, multiskilled operator above other jobs—in part to minimize bumping during layoffs, but instituted no new selection procedures. Accordingly, they ran into problems when the new pay rate for the job attracted 50 bids for the first six positions, many from applicants who lacked the basic verbal and quantitative skills to absorb the training. Because the labor contract mandated training for senior employees who bid on the job, management's only screening option was to spell out the job's multiple duties and encourage self-selection. Though about half the applicants withdrew, the workers who received training were not those who could best absorb it.

The first wave of line operators, who had been allowed to visit vendors and help debug the equipment, were well trained. The operators added for the second shift were not. Moreover, the need for sophisticated training in diagnostic and preventive skills had been badly underestimated. Finally, professional members of the team began to be reassigned elsewhere.

Management coped with this skill gap—which manifested itself in more downtime than had been expected—by taking a variety of temporary actions, some designed to reduce the technical requirements, others intended to augment available capabilities. Management decided, for example, to relax the most complicating technical requirement—the tight interdependence of the system—by creating buffer inventories between an operation that fed a part to the line and the line station that attached it. Within the tub assembly line, management added an in-process queue of 15 semifinished tubs after the work station most likely to go down. These changes, because they implied backing away from characteristics that represented benefits and symbolized the automation discipline, were hotly debated. Some managers feared that these temporary adjustments might be habit forming and become permanent.

Concurrently, management took steps to bolster relevant knowledge and skills. In view of the continuing start-up problems and growing marketplace demand, several dozen professional and technical personnel were brought in from elsewhere in the Major Appliance Business Group to help the project. On the line itself, positions were added and trained operators worked overtime. An interesting reorganization was made in the management structure. A project innovation had combined responsibility for technical support for the manufacturing system with direct supervision in a first-line management position. Six months after the line started, responsibility for technical support was returned to the manufacturing engineering department. As the plant manager explained:

> We backed off because the new product and process created a high load for unit managers and because skilled operators were not fully trained. Moreover, we had to add extra people to a unit in order to keep the line running. I still believe the concept could be made to work—but not in this type of start-up.

Thus, numerous factors conspired to heighten an already demanding technical challenge and to constrain the organization's ability to manage the technical problems. Coping with this skill gap involved scaling down the challenges and bolstering the capabilities. In the concluding section, we draw lessons from how GE managed this skill gap, and how Kendal failed to manage a similar skill gap.

TOWARD MORE SUCCESSFUL
INTRODUCTIONS OF IT

Developing Mastery

An initial gap between the technical requirements of a new IT system and the organizational capabilities needed to manage it is normal (see Figure 8-5). The development of user mastery involves managing the size of the skill (and knowledge) gap. When the skill gap is small, learning occurs slowly. A large gap can be overwhelming, and yield counterproductive frustration. A moderate gap is desirable because it is motivational, drives the learning process, and allows for reinforcing successes.

The gap in both the Kendal and dishwasher projects became overwhelming and counterproductive. In Kendal, the requirements were heightened by introducing the system on top of a consolidation of several service units. Numerous factors depressed the initial capabilities or slowed the learning process. Managers who assumed positions in the new, larger service center had limited or relatively underdeveloped management abilities, and were not supported by temporary additional staff. They refused assistance from outside consultants or corporate personnel, and neglected to provide more than token education and training. The cumulative effect of these circumstances is to slow the development of mastery.

In the dishwasher project, a similarly impressive set of factors initially heightened the technical challenge and depressed capabilities. How the managements of these two cases coped with the excessive capabilities deficit was markedly different. Whereas Kendal management lived with the deficit, GE managers took steps to lower temporarily the requirements and increase organizational capabilities. Some of these actions are especially instructive because they illustrate general steps planners can take to manage the size of the skill gap.

Often, planners can follow a phased introduction of the system to enable mastery of more limited new requirements before the next set is added. In the GE case, management decided to loosen some of the tight couplings in the system which were causing frustrating downtime.

If the technical system is implemented in phases, management can add technical challenge as capabilities develop. This not only helps to keep the skill gap manageable for operating personnel, but also yields a series of smaller successes that may gain the confidence of other interested parties.

Planners should differentiate between the organizational vision for the ongoing operating environment and the organization for start-up. Dishwasher management had to back off the unit manager concept, but probably could have reintroduced it after the most demanding technical challenges had been brought under control and more of the relevant capabilities had been developed. To avoid an excessive deficit in capabilities during introduction, one may also need to assign more people in more specialized roles. It often pays to assign overqualified managers to head such projects, thus permitting the organization to assess as quickly as possible the potential inherent in the technology.

Though this discussion has thus far focused on managing the skill gap during start-up, it is equally important to consider the potential development of a skill surplus, and the opportunity it represents.

Simple forms of automation are installed and stabilized in the spirit of a single declining requirement curve and a single mastery curve. The surplus human capability and the decline in challenge that result can become organizational liabilities to the extent that they lead to boredom and inattention. Management of the dishwasher CIM had the option of treating the system in this way once the original expectations were met. But it could also continue to enhance the manufacturing system, for example, by increasing its flexibility to handle multiple product models without impairing efficiency. Information aspects of the system could also be elaborated and exploited in numerous ways. Expectations of the system could be escalated to take advantage of the growth in human capabilities and, conversely, human learning could be promoted in order to further elaborate the system's capabilities.

Management frequently declares victory too soon, freezing a system and ignoring the potential represented by continual learning. You will recall from Chapter 1 that American manufacturers have failed to develop and exploit the inherent flexibility of FMS technology to produce greater numbers of different parts efficiently. Jaikumar explains this in terms of the failure of developers and managers of these systems in the United States to ensure continual learning.

> A lot of learning takes place in the first two years, when a lot of problems are solved by the vendor and people internal to the organization in task forces. However, when the problems are solved and procedures have been codified, relatively unskilled operators take over the role of machine tending. There is no continual renewal in the use of these skills, as new demands are not placed on the same parts in higher tolerances.[3]

Such practices result in systems that may be well tailored to their present environment but that are incapable of change.

The alternative Jaikumar and others have recommended eschews the very concept of a steady state for IT—the technology can, in the spirit of the "spiral" model of IT development in Figure IV-1, and the succession of curves in Figure 8-5, continue to be elaborated to capture individual and organizational learning and fuel the learning process.

The skill surplus, and the potential for it to develop, present an opportunity in open-ended IT. Increased mastery is used to elaborate the functionality of the system and thereby create a demand for more learning.

Both IT system scenarios—the single maturing curves and the never ending series of new curves—are oversimplifications. But they represent very different visions of IT, and only in the latter does continuous learning become a key element of IT implementation.

Developing Alignment and Ownership

The Kendal system's lack of alignment with the headquarter's business and organization strategies, and its deficiencies in commitment and ownership, derived in part from common oversights. The case illustrates by omissions two principles of managing the introduction of IT systems:

- check and recheck the evolving IT system against the strategic vision; and
- understand the dual potentialities of IT and manage to establish the preferred interpretation.

The Kendal IT system had dual business potentialities. It could be used to increase efficiency; it could be used to augment service quality and marketing. It had dual organizational potentialities: it could be used to increase supervisory control and compliance, or it could be used to expand worker self-management. Because managers neglected to check the evolving system against the vision and didn't understand these dual potentialities, they allowed themselves to fall back on past habits and established priorities. As a result, they focused on efficiency matters rather than service quality or marketing opportunities; hence, the misalignment. Managers.also allowed themselves to be seduced by the power of the system to measure the quantitative aspects of organizational behavior and by their new ability to communicate through the system without physical contact.[4] Their use of the monitoring capability of the system elicited a pattern of defensive responses from subordinates which, if it were allowed to continue unchecked, threatened to completely undermine worker support for the system. Supervisors' use of the system to gain remote control of the field work force rather than to free themselves up in order to spend time in the field with workers and customers was another self-defeating choice between two potentialities of the technology.

In a word, local management failed to establish the priorities called for by the new company vision—for marketing and service and for employee commitment and self-management. In doing so, it undermined field personnel's ownership of the system as well as its overall alignment with company strategies.

Chapter 9—Diffusing IT Systems

The Internal Revenue Service's Automated Examination System (AES) reflected in two of its programs the dual potentialities of IT systems.

> If you're talking about the Workcenter 1040, then [the tax computations and the workpapers] are all built in. The workcenter produces a workpaper that looks identical every time you run the program. It's built in. The numbers and the narrative change, but the basic format is identical.
>
> But with Enable, you're freewheeling. It's like customizing. The agent can do whatever he wants to suit his style. That's why I say that agents like Enable more than the workcenter, because they are free to choose how they want to do it. No two people in my group work alike.
>
> —An IRS trainer[1]

The conformity-promoting "Workcenter 1040" program reinforced the bureaucratic character of the organization. The Enable program, inasmuch as it enhanced revenue agents' sense of autonomy, ran counter to organizational norms. AES thus could, and did, have contrasting meanings for adopters, as we will explore in more detail later.

This chapter treats the role of managing meanings and other factors that affect the diffusion of IT. The meanings users assign to a system influence not only whether the system is aligned with its vision, but also their attitudes toward the system and the way they approach learning about it.

Figure 9-1 summarizes the types of actions that promote diffusion, including experimentation and transfer of technology.

Figure 9-1.   Role of Diffusion Activities in Effective IT Implementation

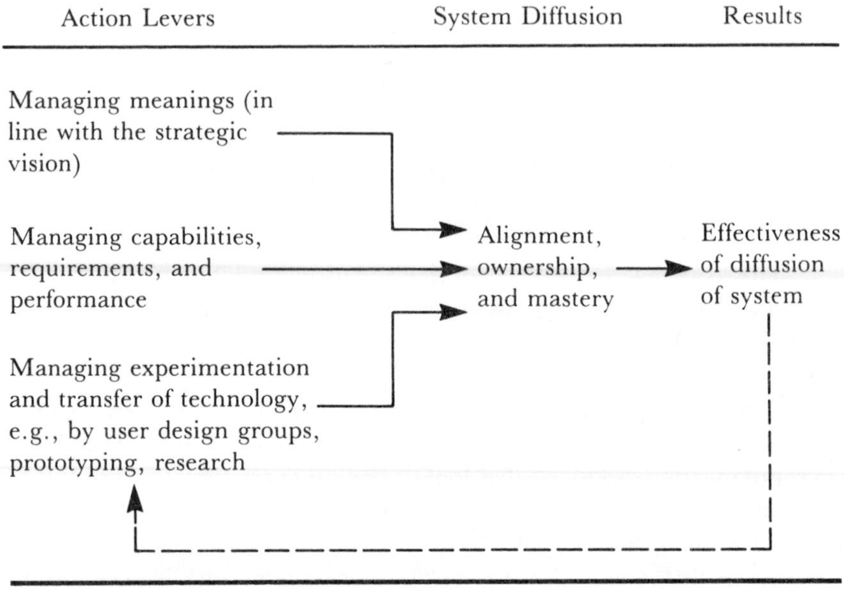

Action Levers	System Diffusion	Results

Managing meanings (in line with the strategic vision)

Managing capabilities, requirements, and performance — Alignment, ownership, and mastery → Effectiveness of diffusion of system

Managing experimentation and transfer of technology, e.g., by user design groups, prototyping, research

Case material in this chapter addresses the diffusion challenge in situations where individual users as well as managers of organizational units must decide whether and how to use a system. One case focuses on the actions taken to spread the XSEL expert system in Digital. It features the iterative character of the development/diffusion process captured by the spiral model of design, try, evaluate, and redesign (see Figure IV-1).

A series of other cases examines contrasting approaches to managing the diffusion of personal computers. These cases, expanding on the quote that opens this chapter, illustrate how manager and user interpretations can lead adopting units to utilize the same basic technology in sharply contrasting ways. Previous chapters have repeatedly emphasized the dual potentialities of IT—how the same basic technology can be used to (1) increase efficiency or improve effectiveness and add value, and (2) ensure employee compliance or elicit employee commitment. These dual potentialities should be recognized, and conscious choices made between them, in formulating a strategic vision (such as AT&T's),

in designing an IT system (such as Allen-Bradley's), and when introducing IT systems (such as the one at Kendal). Not surprisingly, the dual potentialities of IT systems must also be understood and their implications managed in the diffusion process.

DIFFUSING DIGITAL'S XSEL—ITERATIVE WORK ON ALIGNMENT AND SUPPORT

The discussion of design processes in Chapter 7 related how Digital Equipment Corporation sales representatives acted as co-developers for XSEL, the interactive expert system that guided and checked computer system configurations. User involvement not only affected XSEL design in the more formative phases of the project, but also proved to be a factor in eliciting organizational support for the diffusion process. Our interest here is in the relevance of user involvement for diffusion. We are also interested in the various other activities that continued to improve the organization-technology alignment of the system and build support and ownership for it among the user community. Both the alignment and support-generating processes were highly iterative. Leonard-Barton, whose report I drew upon earlier, viewed XSEL as an example of "an interactive process of incrementally altering the technology to fit the organization and simultaneously shaping the user environment to exploit the potential use of the technology."[2]

The early development phase commenced in the spring of 1981 and continued until the summer of 1984, when XSEL was officially sanctioned for wide diffusion. At that time, XSEL users in the United States numbered 234. A year later, there were 396 users, two years later, 769 users. What helped promote the diffusion of XSEL? What retarded it?

Aligning by Prototyping

XSEL's initial development phase was based on the one for the earlier XCON system, an expert system for technical editors in manufacturing. Development of XSEL continued after the process of diffusion was under way, and became increasingly influenced by practical experience with the system.

One mechanism for aligning technology and user environment is prototyping. By introducing XSEL (in its successive forms) into various parts of the organization, the project team was able to learn how the system functioned under various circumstances and how it was used by different sales representatives. For example, did sales representatives use XSEL directly, or did they delegate its use to technical assistants? Did users employ it to guide a configuration from the beginning or to verify a manually designed configuration?

The technical design of these prototypes influenced how XSEL was used, but, equally significant, the patterns of actual usage that came to light in these prototyping experiments influenced subsequent modifications to technical design.

Generating Support by Evidence of Results

Assessing design implications of a prototype is closely related to assessing the system's performance results; both are important for generating further support for the system.

There were several systematic efforts to assess performance contributions of XSEL. One, conducted by a district manager in 1985, required all district sales representatives to run their quotations through XSEL. A performance indicator of the accuracy of system components subsequently improved dramatically. The XSEL project team quickly seized upon the story as a tool for selling the system to would-be adopters but backed off when the results were challenged on various grounds (e.g., the validity of the performance indicator used, political motivation of the district manager). Another study, by technical editors in Scotland, carefully tested XSEL's accuracy through 1,000 runs. Experimentation with various techniques for increasing the accuracy of scores identified three minor but common problems that, when corrected, increased the accuracy score from 75% to 90%. This evidence of XSEL's utility was convincing, and played a role in generating support in the user community.

Creating the Support of Gatekeepers

In 1982, the project team won support from a vice president of sales. The source of support backfired when this strategic gatekeeper to the sales organization, by his enthusiasm, elicited an agreement from the team that it could not reasonably have been expected to keep. The developers agreed, in September 1982, to have XSEL ready by Christmas for every sales district that wanted it. In fact, this several months grew to two years, and the team was widely criticized for overselling and underperforming. "High visibility can be worse than none at all if the timing is wrong," concludes Leonard-Barton.[3]

Another lesson Leonard-Barton illustrates with XSEL is the importance of identifying and working with different individuals or groups as they become critical to the diffusion path. For example, during one period, systems managers who managed machine usage in each of seven regions became critical to the diffusion of XSEL. The seven managers ranged widely in their willingness to move other programs around to make room for XSEL, requiring the team to spend time convincing the more skeptical of them about the soundness of XSEL and reassuring the more sympathetic that productivity benefits would follow.

The most critical "battle to preserve XSEL" occurred in a meeting requested by the project team in which it described XSEL and its performance benefits to a central committee of top sales managers. The enthusiasm and credibility of the highly regarded sales representatives who served on the development team carried the day at this meeting, resulting in official approval for the diffusion of XSEL.

Getting the Technical System Right

Leonard-Barton observes that technology development teams frequently underestimate the importance of the delivery system and other aspects of the technical infrastructure. The adequacy of the technical aspects of XSEL and the system for delivering it were clearly important for both alignment and support. For example, XSEL's response time suffered when the computer or communication system was loaded, affecting both how the system was used and how much support it received from users. Poor response time weakened support for the system and probably contributed to a tendency for sales representatives to delegate XSEL use to technical assistants.

The development team achieved gradual improvement in the quality of the delivery system from 1983, but not until 1986 did it gain control of this factor so critical to the effective diffusion of XSEL. In the meantime, it persuaded the hot line center that serviced other internal Digital software to support XSEL, and convinced the sales training program to include a module on the system.

In summary, many management levers were employed to influence the diffusion of XSEL. Its alignment with the organization was achieved by involving users in the design group and employing the prototyping technique. The support of the user community was garnered by eliciting user involvement, by improving system response time and the technical delivery system, and by providing evidence of system performance. Mastery was enhanced by training and hot line support. These factors are summarized in Figure 9-2, which also conveys the extent to which their influence involved iterative cycles of action—diffusion, action, and more diffusion.

PCs FOR ACCOUNTANTS IN TWO COMPANIES—CONTRASTING MEANINGS AND USAGE

Two companies studied by Carroll and Perin introduced and diffused personal computers into their accounting functions, experiencing contrasting patterns of utilization.[4] These differences in usage resulted from contrasting visions and different implementation activities. In explaining how management words and actions

Figure 9-2.   Factors Influencing Diffusion of XSEL in Digital
                   Equipment Corporation

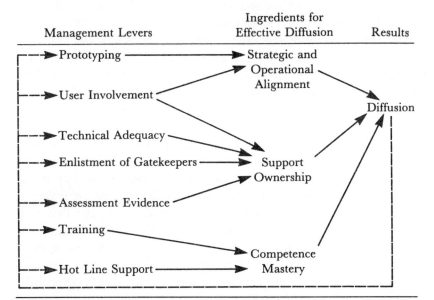

Note: Feedback from diffusion outcomes to management levers reflects the iterative nature of the prototyping and other processes required to develop and
diffuse XSEL. It also indicates that some diffusion success preceded and enabled
certain management actions such as assessments, hot line diagnostic support, and
the enlistment of critical gatekeepers.

influenced the adoption and use of IT tools, the authors underscore the importance of expectations.

One of these companies derived modest benefit from the personal computers. The Resource Company, which engaged in
large-scale exploration and marketing of natural resources, introduced PCs to help its accounting group of several hundred
keep track of the revenues and taxes associated with thousands of
leases of varying sizes. Carroll and Perin concluded that after a
couple of years the microcomputers "had found a useful niche in
accountants' work processes." Most users reported time savings in
performing old tasks but described their work content as essen-
tially unchanged. About 20% said that the time freed up by the

PCs was used to find problems and do more in-depth analyses. Some reported taking on new responsibilities, but others were concerned that the PCs were being overused. In general, the use of the PCs appeared to have topped out.

Benefits derived by the other company, Commco, were significantly more impressive. Part of a large telecommunications corporation, Commco introduced PCs into two groups totaling 200 employees. Reduced drudgery and considerable savings in time were reported after two years. The reduction of repetitive tasks had enabled the company to redesign some jobs. Previously fragmented work was combined into whole tasks, increasing the meaning of the work. Time saved was being reinvested in exploration, analysis, and "what if" simulations, thereby providing management with a wider range of information for decision making. Commco users expressed far greater enthusiasm for the PCs and their impact on their jobs than Resource employees; indeed, a few Commco clerks had already experienced new career opportunities.

Why the difference in results? The explanation began, appropriately, with differences in the technology visions.

Visions: Automate versus Informate

The management sponsor at Resource saw the PC as a "fancy adding machine," a stand-alone tool capable of automating spreadsheets and benefiting the business primarily by increasing efficiency. He did not appear to have any particular hopes or expectations about coordinated organizational change.

Management sponsors at Commco acknowledged that PCs would automate certain activities, but emphasized their informating capabilities. The PCs were viewed within the framework of a more ambitious and more strategic vision, embracing IT functions and business benefits explicitly and organizational change implicitly. Early uses included spreadsheets, data-based work, word processing, and decision support; in future, PCs would become part of an integrated process, linked to the corporate Commco mainframe and distributed minis. Implicit in this vision was a work force with upgraded skills.

But visions by themselves only guide; they do not determine the actions taken to introduce and diffuse IT systems.

Diffusion Strategies: Control versus Facilitate

Just as they were at variance in their visions, the managements at Resource and Commco employed different activities to diffuse their PCs. Resource activities emphasized prescribing and controlling the use of the IT tools. Training was self-initiated and, beyond an introductory session and a one-hour-per-week allowance, occurred on one's own time. Anyone could suggest or develop spreadsheet applications, but would receive no particular support for doing so. The manager who sponsored the PCs proscribed their use for writing analyses; memos were to continue to be sent to the word-processing pool. Neither the group manager nor the supervisors modeled the frequent use of computers.

Diffusion activities at Commco sent more encouraging and supportive signals to potential users. A simple procedure was established for ordering PCs and relevant software. In-house computer education was offered to employees at all levels of the organization. Broad encouragement was given to the development of applications; skilled PC users were placed in many areas and given responsibility for developing applications and helping other users.

Management's vision shaped its implementation activities, and these activities shaped the meaning of the PCs for employees. These meanings or expectations became, in turn, self-fulfilling (see Figure 9-3). Resource viewed the PC as a limited-purpose tool, implemented it in a risk-averse way, with just enough education to automate, and produced modest results that soon plateaued. Commco viewed PCs as "offering a set of capabilities whose realization depends on the ingenuity of vendors, software developers, users," and so forth. Its program initiated significant organizational change, and realized increased potentialities and expanding results.

*Figure 9-3. The Sources and Consequences of Meanings Attributed to PCs
in Resource and Commco*

Management Actions	Meanings and Implications for Alignment, Ownership, and Mastery	Diffusion Outcomes
Resource IT vision: automate Training: left to individual Support for software innovations: little Procedures: proscribe certain uses	Meaning of PCs: a limited-purpose tool Alignment: yes Ownership: moderate Mastery: bounded	Time saved, but few value-added uses Usage topped out No organizational change
Commco IT vision: informate Training: major effort in classroom and OJT Support for software innovations: strong Procedures: facilitate acquisition and usage of PC and software	Meaning of PCs: a bundle of capabilities to be developed Alignment: yes Ownership: high Mastery: continually expanding	Time saved and reallocated to more value-added activities Continuous development of uses Organizational change

PCs FOR IRS AGENTS—MORE ON HOW
MEANINGS ARE SHAPED

In the first phase of its Automated Examination System (AES), between July 1986 and the end of 1987, the IRS distributed laptop PCs, software, and training to more than 14,000 revenue agents, who were encouraged, but not required, to use the new tool. Pentland's investigation of this implementation extends our understanding of how meanings are shaped by management actions.[5] His analysis suggests that IRS managers' support for learning activities and the development of "software communities" among subordinates affected the diffusion of end-user computing.

Revenue agents conduct field audits of businesses and high-dollar individuals. The subjects of these audits and the tasks of the auditors are highly varied. Agents must continually decide what data to go after, and gather them in ways appropriate to the situation. They must research the laws, analyze data, compute and sell adjustments, and file reports on resolved and unresolved cases.

The IRS was guided by a vision of automating the process to save labor, increase the accessibility of records, and improve quality control. The introduction of laptops was to be the first of several phases. Planned follow-on phases included: establishing a national network with larger computers; providing legal guidance; on-line access to records; and applying artificial intelligence to classify and select returns for various purposes. The IT vision included performance objectives—reduced cost, higher quality, and greater consistency in applying the tax code. To my knowledge, the IRS had not articulated a vision of future organization to guide the development of IT for revenue agents or other units of the agency.

Agents' laptops were provided with two main programs for analysis and report writing mentioned at the beginning of this chapter. The AES project office had developed the Workcenter 1040 as a comprehensive tool for auditing 1040 returns. Legal research and other menu items were to be added later as the program became one piece of a hierarchical network of computing power. The other program, called "Enable," was a commercial package that provided word-processing, spreadsheet, database, and communications capabilities. Tax-related applications programs and templates could be written for Enable.

Actual benefits derived by agents who made significant use of the laptop computers included time savings, a more disciplined approach to analysis and documentation, and more professional appearing documentation. Some felt that being equipped with the computer impressed taxpayers and enhanced their professional stature.

Hardware and software issued to agents was identical; training, learning time, and other forms of support provided by managers varied from location to location. According to a management agreement with the agents' union, agents could not be evaluated on their use of laptop computers during the introductory phase.

Pentland's investigation comprised two studies: an interview study of four districts; and a questionnaire study of approximately 1,000 revenue agents throughout the system.

Contrasting Actions in Four Districts—Implications for Mastery and Ownership

Two of the districts in Pentland's interview study (A and B) showed generally low use of the laptops, two (C and D) generally high use. The high-use districts were characterized by (1) high-quality, on-the-job training (timely, generous, and supplied by attentive instructors); (2) rumors supporting the idea that laptop use would become mandatory at the conclusion of the 18-month trial period; (3) the emergence of an active local software community that supported the development and sharing of templates, worksheets, and so forth; and (4) generally supportive attitudes toward AES.

These characteristics were absent in the low-use districts. Districts A and B allotted less time to OJT, and the instructor, a peer agent, was not available in a timely manner. Agents could not begin to use new skills acquired in the classroom before losing them through disuse. Neither beliefs nor norms developed to augment the individual agent's motivation to use the laptop. Not surprisingly, less support and ownership for AES developed among agents in districts A and B.

Why did these differences emerge in a large bureaucratic agency that prizes and promotes uniformity and consistency? We can begin to see in Figure 9-4 that IRS district managers, like the managers at Resource and Commco, had shaped the meaning of IT for users.

Managers in districts C and D had made a convincing case that it was okay to invest the extra time in casework in order to learn how to make productive use of the laptop. Observed one agent: "The management has said that time is no problem as long as you're working and learning. Time on case is on the back burner. There is historically a strong emphasis on time, so this is unusual."[6]

Managers in districts A and B, while publicly espousing the official policy of allowing agents to take the extra time needed to learn, also reflected their ambivalence. Agents in district B felt they needed approval from their group managers to take the extra time on a case to learn how to use the computer. "You have to force yourself to use the computer right now," said one.

> It really doesn't save any time at first. They tell you that you have all the time in the world to do these exams with the PC, but in practice it doesn't work out that way. After the exam they'll ask, "Why all the hours on that exam?" and it really doesn't help to say, "Because I used the PC." The pressure is always on to keep the hours down and the yield up.[7]

District managers' actions also influenced development of a supportive community. In districts C and D, managers actively encouraged grassroots innovations (e.g., user development and sharing of templates). They recognized agents' contributions and officially sanctioned meetings to swap innovations. In contrast, managers in districts A and B tried to control applications. To ensure their accuracy and avoid duplication of effort, they required software to be reviewed by a district committee, and discouraged informal sharing.

Figure 9-4.   The Sources and Consequences of Meanings Attributed to AES in IRS Districts A and B versus C and D

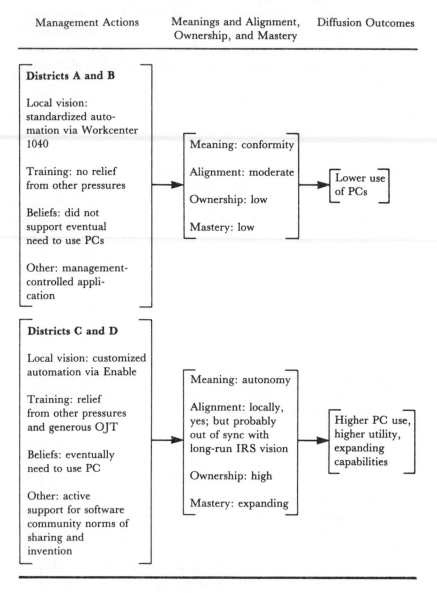

The constructive syndrome found by Pentland in districts C and D but not in districts A and B is summarized in Figure 9-5. The diagrammatic interpretation of the C and D pattern efficiently portrays its syndrome character. The feedback effects are especially important in understanding the cumulative nature of positive attitudes and usage and, conversely, of negative attitudes and nonusage.

Questionnaire Study—A Matter of Alignment of IT with Business Purpose

Comparison of the findings of the four-district interview study with the results of the larger questionnaire survey (which did not include the districts interviewed) yields some additional insights into the AES implementation effort.

Figure 9-5.   Constructive Syndrome of Management Actions, User Response, and Utilization of IT in IRS Districts C and D

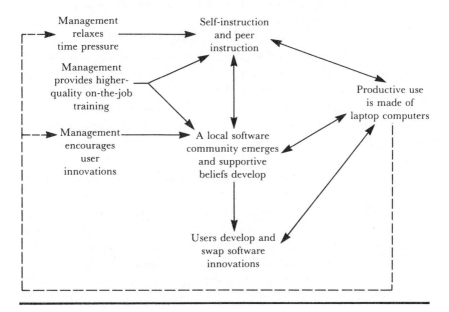

The survey study employed three implementation success indicators: reported levels of use, user satisfaction, and productivity.

- Use—65% of the agents surveyed reported that they "currently use" the laptop 10 hours or more a week; half say they use it 20 hours or more a week.
- Satisfaction—78% of the agents agree that "the laptop is an appropriate tool for Revenue Agents."
- Productivity—15% of the agents reported that "on the whole, the laptop reduces time on the case." About 70% said that the laptop allowed them to do some things faster; an equal number reported that they sometimes used it for work they could do faster by hand.

Implementation was thus successful in terms of use and user satisfaction, but not productivity, which was the driving rationale for AES. Pentland considered that the low percentage of agents who reported improvements might reflect the relative inexperience of users at the time of the study, but he failed to find a correlation between length of time agents had used the tool and reports on productivity improvement. He concluded that the more likely interpretation was that the technology was a poor fit for the tax-auditing task.

Why the extensive use of an IT system that might be poorly aligned to the productivity goal? First, as the satisfaction finding suggests, users must have liked it for other reasons. Some may have enjoyed the process of mastering the new tool, especially Enable users who became members of an active software community. Others might have appreciated the improved appearance of their documents and the positive effect on their professional image.

Second, even though use was officially discretionary, some agents felt obliged to use the laptop. In districts C and D, where management assumed a supportive stance, the belief that laptop use would eventually be made mandatory tended to reinforce a positive pattern, including satisfaction with the system. In the larger sample, the agents' belief that laptop use would soon be required correlated positively with use but negatively with productivity and satisfaction. Obviously, managers in many locations encouraged agents who were otherwise skeptical of the laptop's utility to believe that use would soon become mandatory.

A Future Alignment Issue for IRS

The IRS case also illustrates a type of tension that stood to be exacerbated by the high-usage patterns of districts C and D. Active usage patterns involved the Enable software rather than the Workcenter 1040 program. As the opening paragraphs of this chapter signaled, the meanings attached to these two programs contrasted sharply.

For users in districts C and D who adopted Enable, the laptop afforded a degree of autonomy in an otherwise heavily bureaucratic context. But at higher levels of the IRS hierarchy, local invention and the diversity it created was viewed as anathema or at best a passing phase. At this organizational level, standardized programming for Workcenter 1040 was held to be the ideal, not only because it suited the IRS's preferences for control, but also because it directly served the need to ensure as much consistency as possible in the treatment of individual taxpayers.

TOWARD MORE EFFECTIVE DIFFUSION EFFORTS

The cases reviewed in this chapter illustrate the importance of managing many different factors during the diffusion of IT systems.

To promote mastery, management must ensure adequacy of training, technical support, and organizational support. Recall, for example:

- Digital's hot line support for XSEL;
- Commco's generous classroom and on-the-job training; and
- the relief from other performance pressures and active support for software community norms of invention and sharing in IRS districts C and D.

To promote ownership, management can build social support, provide evidence of results, and commit technical resources. Recall, for example:

- Digital's involvement of users and enlistment of gatekeepers, upgrading of the technical delivery system, and promulgation of evidence of results; and
- Commco's facilitating procedures that enabled users to acquire PCs and software and afforded the latitude to use them.

To promote alignment, management can engage in the kind of prototyping employed by Digital. Additionally, and more important, given the alternative interpretations of PC technology, management should consciously attempt to shape the meanings individuals attach to it. The Resource, Commco, and IRS-AES cases all reinforce the idea that management must influence meanings. Indeed, it should plan in terms of the hypotheses that people carry around in their heads about the probable meaning the system has for them. It should ask, "What do we want the system to mean to users?" and "What do we want users to expect from the system?" Management must think through how its actions to diffuse IT tools will influence meanings. It must be sensitive to the meanings that emerge and attempt to understand the factors that are shaping them.

To promote the type of learning that will lead to full utilization of an informating technology, management must ensure that it goes beyond training operators in the ABCs of accessing and using the system and provides an opportunity for exploration and experimentation. Support for such learning was provided by Commco but not Resource.

How management handles the introduction of IT, including training, helps shape its meaning for users. At Commco the following management actions and stances promoted a view of the PC as an unbounded capability whose contributions depended upon individual ingenuity and cumulative learning:

- generous amounts of time freed up for learning;
- support and encouragement for inventing and sharing software; and

- strategic placement of expert users with responsibility for helping their peers.

Many of the activities related in earlier cases helped shape meanings of IT in a strategic way. Recall management's overtures to the union in the GE dishwasher case, the involvement of paper machinery operators (but not their supervisors) in the ETS case, and the use of words like "integration" and "architecture" and the presence of corporate staff (but not business representatives) in the meeting with members of International Metal's executive committee (which was anxious that the IT systems not reverse its decentralization policy). Managing meanings is an important aspect of all phases of the extended implementation processes, but it plays a crucial role in the introduction and diffusion stages.

Chapter 10—Conclusion—Key
Implementation Issues

The theory about integrating IT and the organization advanced in this book can be summarized thusly: implementation effectiveness depends crucially upon (1) good direction (embracing, in particular, an alignment of business, technology, and organization strategies); (2) high organizational commitment, stakeholder support, and ownership; and (3) strong competence in general, and user mastery in particular.

These ingredients take on increasing specificity as implementation progresses. For example, concern about an aligned strategic framework in Phase One gives way to attention to an integrated IT/organizational system in Phase Two, and then to operational alignment during introduction and diffusion. Similarly, general commitment and competence are important contextual conditions for developing IT systems, but need to be translated into user ownership and mastery of a particular system in Phase Three. Actions influence these ingredients within any given phase, and earlier phases of the process influence conditions in later phases. Chapters 3 through 9 presented and discussed specific propositions covering these multiple relationships. Figure 10-1 summarizes the thrust of these hypotheses and illustrates their relationships with one another.

Threading through the phase-by-phase treatment of the process are several issues that warrant further discussion. The first issue is the timing for addressing organizational matters. At what stage in the implementation process is it both desirable and feasible to make organizational choices? The second is participation. Which users and other stakeholders can be involved effectively, in what

Figure 10-1. *Summary Framework of Theory and Practice for Effective IT Implementation*

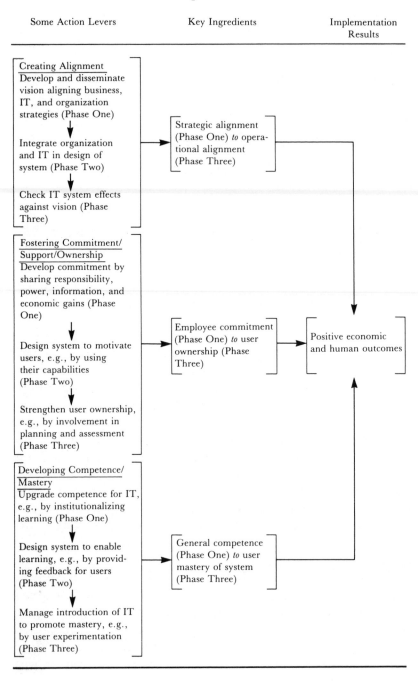

capacities, and at what point in the process? The third is assessment. How can we learn how well implementation is proceeding? The fourth is leadership. What can be expected from leadership contributions, and when are they most crucial? In the spirit of developing a practical theory of implementation, I will frame the answers to these questions as propositions—ones that specify the considerations that should influence planners' choices.

ADDRESSING ORGANIZATIONAL ASPECTS OF AN INTEGRATED IT SYSTEM—WHEN?

When in the extended implementation process should planners attempt to develop the organizational aspects of IT systems? There are three options:

1. anticipatory development of the organization (mostly in Phase One);
2. simultaneous development of technology and the organization (in Phases Two and Three); and
3. reactive-adaptive development of the organization (late in Phase Three).

The first option, anticipatory development of the organization, cannot be thought of as a total strategy. Certainly, early alignment of broad organization strategy with business and technology strategies is desirable and often feasible. The discussion of the IBM Raleigh case in Chapter 4 identified many contextual conditions of the organization which management can develop in advance. It can take steps to share power, responsibility, information, status, and economic gains in order to create employee commitment, and can employ various devices to institutionalize continuous learning. Often, aspects of the organizational infrastructure which are more tailored to future IT systems can be put in place in advance of the design of these systems, in effect adapting the technology to the organization, as in the decentralization of manufacturing in Kodak. We thus argue that management can increase its efforts to identify and improve general organizational conditions favorable to IT.

The third option—adapting the organization after the fact—is still the prevalent practice. The traditional technology-driven change strategy is an extreme version of this reactive-adaptive option. Relying upon the technology to automatically produce the appropriate organizational response often leads to poor technology design and unintended organizational responses (recall the telephone answering center repair bureau and the Kendal project), but sound reasons may exist for deferring certain organizational design issues until the technology is introduced. Planners may, for example, be unable to anticipate the appropriate organization structure, pay scheme, or performance management strategy. Although planners of the decision-support system for papermaking should have given earlier attention to the supervisory role, they probably would have been unable to actually redesign the role in advance of experience with the new system. Even when planners can anticipate the organization, doing so may overload the design and the early introduction processes.

Although the reactive-adaptive option is common practice, the simultaneous development of organization and technology (option 2) is advocated in the current academic literature on IT development. This option, well illustrated by Shell's Sarnia chemical plant design, Kodak's workshop technique, and DEC's XSEL system, allows organizational and technology choices to influence one another. Assuming management has done what it can to improve the organizational context, IT systems planners should address many of the organizational and technology design issues jointly. But we need better ways to think about when it is both desirable and feasible to do so.

I propose the following considerations relative to timing the development of organizational components of an integrated system.

1. Does the company in question already have an organizational philosophy, a clear organizational change agenda covering issues such as centralization-decentralization, individualism-teamwork, uniformity-diversity? To cite some examples, Kodak, Thorn EMI's rental group, and the APC paper company each had a strong philosophy of pushing decision making to the lowest level at which information and expertise could be provided. *The more*

strongly the leadership has committed itself to an organizational philosophy, the more desirable it is for planners to develop organization and technology simultaneously.

2. Are there many rather than one or a few different technical configurations, each with its own unique set of human and organizational implications, available to solve the business problem? Earlier information technologies were relatively deterministic; for example, batch processing central mainframes automated routine functions and invariably created simple data entry jobs. On-line distributed and integrated processing is more flexible and allows for more IT/organization options. The Automated Examination System developed by the IRS for revenue agents was introduced with two different configurations. The Workcenter 1040 application, a highly programmed system in which agents simply entered figures and cranked out results, reinforced the agency's bureaucratic control culture. The Enable application, which allowed agents to develop their own tools, tended to promote autonomy. The fact that the IRS system could be configured in different ways, each with its own meaning, made it advantageous to confront the implicit organizational choice early in the implementation process. *The more technical flexibility that exists in using IT to serve the business requirements, the more desirable is simultaneous development of IT and organization.*

3. Are the organizational conditions that will eventually complement the technology necessary to achieve even minimally satisfactory results, or are they necessary only to fully realize the potential of the technology? Recall the progressive degradation of the medical records system discussed in Chapter 1; doctors and clerks did not enter data into it, and the doctors would not use it because the electronic records were incomplete. The system's planners should have addressed the question of organizational incentives up front, but they did not. *The more that even initially satisfactory results depend upon implementing the complementary organizational conditions, the more urgent is simultaneous development.*

4. Can the complementary organization be as readily implemented after the introduction of the technology? Management sometimes makes an IT investment contingent upon union agreement to flexible practices. If management does not take advantage

of this window of opportunity, it may find it difficult, if not impossible, to negotiate the needed change later. Even if formal agreement is not required, the unfreezing of attitudes and expectations can create a window of opportunity for designing and implementing change.

Self-perpetuating dynamics established early in the life of an implemented IT system can make subsequent organizational development difficult. Paper machine supervisors claimed control of the Expense Tracking System during its first year of operation, and operators responded with "You want it? It's yours!" Such antagonistic dynamics have a life of their own; usually, they are more easily avoided than resolved. Self-perpetuating behavior patterns also developed around the laptops introduced in four IRS districts. In half of the districts, development of a positive syndrome supported effective use of the laptops; in the other half, negative syndromes limited their use.

The more difficult it will be to achieve the preferred organizational pattern after the introduction of technology or after an unwanted organizational pattern has developed, the more effort planners should make to pursue a simultaneous development strategy.

5. Can planners forecast on the basis of experience, research, or theory the types of organizational and technology choices that are likely to match one another? Based on a review of the NRC study findings and the experiences of other CIM installations, I believe it is possible to anticipate the organizational and technology choices for CIM systems. Arrangements for home-based professionals supported by IT networks, on the other hand, may be so diverse that one can't anticipate the appropriate organization.

Planners may also not be able to forecast many of the organizational implications of technologies such as electronic messaging and teleconferencing, which are still in early stages of development, because the problems and opportunities that emerge may be unique to each organization. For example, a problem with junk mail may develop in one organization but not in another. We do know that new norms must be developed to regulate use and avoid abuse. *The more familiar the form of IT in question, the greater the number of organizational issues planners can develop simultaneously with the technology.*

6. Do motivation and legitimacy exist for organizational development in general, and for considering the full range of organization options? At Citibank Brazil, organizational development apparently was not a legitimate topic for planning and discussion. In situations where home-based work might be an organizational solution, the basic premises of this arrangement are so radical that the option is not usually considered. Although ideally the climate should be supportive, in practice planners must take the existence of organizational blinders into account. *The more favorable the climate for considering organizational options, the more feasible it is for planners to commit to simultaneous development.*

7. Are the *resources*—time, energy, and dollars—available for early organizational development? Simultaneous development of technology and organization can sometimes overload the design process.

Systems developers argue, with justification, that the technology development process is already complex enough without trying to address social criteria and organizational design issues at the same time. Projects are typically already behind schedule and over budget. Moreover, developers are concerned that if managers anticipated and confronted at the outset all of the organizational implications of technology, they might not go ahead with the proposed technology.

Managers of prospective users often argue that even if organization and technology could be designed jointly, introducing new roles, structures, rewards, and authority relations when the technology is installed would overload the user organization. The management of the GE dishwasher project, for example, had to back away from the new unit manager concept during the start-up because the temporary heavy workload required more managerial personnel, not fewer.

Thus, the more organizational slack available for designing and introducing new systems, the more feasible it is for planners to commit to simultaneous development.

Planners weight heavily, perhaps too heavily, an additional consideration—tactical considerations lead them to minimize discussion of a proposed system among stakeholders and/or to justify it in ways that do not reflect their real intentions. This was illustrated in the discussion of the selection and approval of systems in the aerospace company. Thomas identified several tactical reasons why sponsors in Aerospace tried to keep it quiet: to avoid border wars with departments that might oppose the IT system or want to modify it; to avoid discussions with the union, which might slow down the process; and to avoid closer scrutiny of the optimistic staffing assumptions contained in the proposal. He also found that sponsors sometimes tailored the framing of the benefits of a proposed system to the particular concerns of their superiors rather than to other purposes more strategic to the company.

The less these tactical considerations enter into the process, the more stakeholders can influence the organizational aspects of the IT system.

MANAGING PARTICIPATION— WHO, WHEN, AND WHY?

What type of participation in the extended implementation process will enhance its effectiveness? Breadth of participation refers to the inclusion of users, other stakeholders, and organizational specialists, along with the sponsors and technical specialists who are inevitably involved in the development process. Depth of participation relates to influencing approval decisions, design choices, training modules, installation and diffusion plans, and assessments of prototypes and pilots.

The amount of participation planners may opt for ranges from the minimal scenario, in which designers ask users for task information they can employ in designing a system, to scenarios that involve deep participation by users and organizational specialists in all aspects of the process, and broad participation (including other stakeholders) in some aspects of the process.

The cases in this book reflect a wide range of participation scenarios—from little or no participation in the telephone company's answering center to substantial participation in Digital's XSEL system, Rolls-Royce's purchase invoice system, Shell's Sarnia chemical plant, and Kodak's workshop technique. Digital, in particular, fostered deep participation by XSEL users, who were involved in developing designs, prototyping and assessing the results, and winning the system's approval. Kodak's workshop technique is impressive for the scope of participation it provides, at least during the initial stages of a project. Participants include users, other stakeholders, and an organizational development specialist. Rolls-Royce and Shell included union representatives in some design and planning processes. Numerous factors, reflecting both what is feasible and desirable, influence the optimal participation scenario for a specific situation.

First, the broad feasibility consideration: *in general, the stronger the skills, attitudes, norms, and established techniques that support participation in an organizational context, the more feasible it is to provide for broad and deep participation in a particular IT project.* Sponsors are more likely to perceive participation as a normal aspect of the process; technical specialists are more likely to have developed an acceptance of the additional complexity of their own work; and all participants are more likely to feel comfortable and confident in the process. The recent trend toward high-commitment management strategies, reported in Chapter 4, has tended to improve the feasibility of participation in IT development.

Second, the broad desirability consideration: *the wider the scope and more significant the probable human implications of the system, the more desirable it is to provide for broad and deep participation.* Chapter 1 summarized, and the other chapters illustrated, how the more profound human implications of advanced IT increase the desirability of participation. The desirability of participation relates to the several functions it performs, and the importance of each function is increased by advanced IT.

One function of participation is *to improve the quality of design and installation planning* by incorporating the best task and organizational knowledge in these activities. Advanced IT increases the complexity of the relationship between the user organization and technology and thus heightens the need for user task expertise and the expertise of organizational development specialists.

A second function of participation is *to generate user support and ownership for the system and the introduction process.* Many forms of advanced IT—those which informate the organization rather than merely automate certain task functions—depend more heavily upon internalized motivation and mental skills, thereby increasing the importance of user support and ownership.

A third function of participation is *to increase the legitimacy and credibility of the process beyond the user group.* The wider organizational scope of the implications of advanced IT increases the importance of legitimacy function.

ASSESSING ALIGNMENT, OWNERSHIP, AND MASTERY—HOW? BY WHOM?

Assessment has traditionally referred first to documenting the economic benefits of the system and second to identifying whether the technical aspects of the system perform as intended. Rarely is a comparable effort made to assess whether the organizational aspects of the system are functioning well. The decision-support system for controlling costs in the papermaking process is a case in point. Management documented the operating improvement and cost reductions attributable to ETS, but did not assess the organizational aspects of the system. It did not consider whether dynamics set in motion by ETS might account for system results plateauing and operator utilization dropping off. Management was fortunate in this instance because case researchers analyzed the organizational aspects of the system and their effects on performance.

The centralized telephone answering facility also dramatized the need for comprehensive and timely assessment. I observed that the manager primarily responsible for implementing the system was shaken when he heard service representatives talk about how certain features of the system had stripped their work of meaning and undermined their self-esteem. Until then, he had assumed that morale problems in the center, and the business costs of these problems, were attributable to supervision. Management should have relied upon a regular assessment process to identify what in this case it learned only because an organizational researcher happened on the scene.

Assessment should include multiple criteria. In addition to

evaluating business results and indexes of technical performance, managers should assess the operational system in terms of the key ingredients of effectiveness. How well is the system aligned with the vision for it? To what extent has ownership for the system developed among users? How much mastery have users developed?

It is also important to take an analytic view of the data gathered. Social, technical, and economic data often need to be analyzed together to explain important outcomes, whether the outcome is a disappointing reduction in staff, a failure to use the flexibility inherent in the technology, or an increased rate of turnover among operating personnel.

The type of assessment I am proposing here is best illustrated by the Kendal case, which is summarized in Figure 8-3. Recall that the analysis of the Kendal project after one year began by assessing alignment, ownership/commitment, and mastery (shown in righthand column of Figure 8-3), and then attempted to find explanations for the strengths and weaknesses in each ingredient. After identifying the more approximate causes (listed in middle column of the diagnostic framework), I attempted to dig deeper to find underlying explanations for the strengths and weaknesses exhibited in this case. The Kendal assessment would be even more instructive if it included a fourth column on the right side of the framework containing business results.

Ideally, such assessments as the Kendal analysis should be performed collaboratively, involving systems specialists, organizational experts, and user representatives. If these several perspectives are brought to bear, the assessment is more likely to be comprehensive and balanced, and it is also more likely to be acted upon.

I envision assessment not only as a vehicle for adjusting a particular system, but also as a means for learning how to improve the design and introduction of future systems. The detailed assessment of the Kendal project, for example, was used as a vehicle for educating top management in the THEi organization about some aspects of the extended implementation process discussed in this book. The purpose was to enable these managers to play a leadership role in creating the context for effective IT implementation.

Assessment should attend equally to explaining the achievements and shortfalls of systems. The need to understand the source of a shortfall is obvious—we have to know what needs to be fixed. The need to understand the source of success is less often acknowleged. Yet a pilot project may be successful for reasons that are partly overlooked by the planners when they set out to institutionalize or diffuse a new IT system. Allen-Bradley's first CIM, for example, was developed and started with project leadership, project personnel, and operating crew members who were the best a highly selective process could identify. Future projects could not count on the same advantage. Pilot projects are often accompanied by a commitment to wide participation and dynamic interaction between users and specialists which produces extremely high motivation and deep learning about the internal workings of the system. When planners review the results of the pilot and consider how to efficiently introduce the system in other locations, they invariably eliminate or shrink drastically the role of participation. Sometimes, the lesser amount of participation in subsequent implementation effort results in a failure to achieve the ownership and depth of knowledge required for the system to work. If planners understand both why a pilot system works as well as it does and how it might be improved, they are more likely to anticipate the full gamut of social and logistical requirements.

PROVIDING LEADERSHIP: AT ALL LEVELS AND THROUGHOUT THE PROCESS

Leadership is reflected in many of the examples of good practice described in this book. It plays an important role in each phase of the implementation process.

During the first phase of the extended implementation process, leadership needs to come from the top of the organization, preferably from the chief executive officer or chief operating officer. Leadership at this stage involves formulating and communicating a long-term vision of where the company is going and how it will get there. The clearest example of this is provided by Jim Maxmin, the CEO of Thorn EMI's rental business, who formulated a vision that covered all three corners of the strategic triangle. Maxmin also took personal charge of a management process that began to disseminate the vision and attend to its implications for system development priorities.

This display of good leadership practice by top management occurred in late 1987; the earlier project at Kendal illustrates failures in leadership at several levels. We observed that the installed system was out of alignment both with business priorities and with organizational philosophy. The operating company executive whose organization included Kendal must bear some responsibility for not having provided to the design team a clearer translation of the newly formulated vision. The Kendal managers, in part in response to pressures of the reward system, concentrated on operations to the neglect of the project's organizational learning objectives. Some responsibility for not relieving the pressure on the experimental unit and ensuring that normal measures and rewards did not undermine both the learning objectives and a marketing and service emphasis accrues to the Kendal manager's immediate superior. Finally, the Kendal manager failed to comprehend the need for assistance in managing the organizational aspects of the pilot installation. Thus, responsibility for the shortcomings of the Kendal project was shared by all levels of management. But more important, the responsible managers were open to learning from their mistakes. All of them participated with interest and without defensiveness in the critique of Kendal stimulated by the Harvard case study.

The GE dishwasher case illustrates the need for leadership throughout the extended implementation process and at several organizational levels. Group executive Schipke personally acted to generate a favorable climate for IT implementation in the management organization, in union-management relations, and on the plant floor. His leadership continued to be critical during the start-up and the transition to full production. He was credited with showing an enabling amount of faith in the subordinates in charge, even as problems developed and dragged the project behind schedule. Another leader, the development project manager, focused continued attention on the original design intentions when problems developed, and guaranteed that the relevant expertise would be brought to bear on the problems. A third leader, the dishwasher plant manager, figured importantly in the successful project. Sometimes in creative tension with the project leader, the plant manager saw to it that practical problems were identified and addressed. He managed the uncertain processes of debugging and starting up the equipment, ensuring that human resource requirements were understood and met, and coping with the pressures of unexpected demand for the new product—under the pressure of his boss's public promise of a successful start-up.

The plant manager's comments on the start-up period indicate the leadership requirement that was placed on him. Describing the enormous operational pressure and anxiety he and his organization experienced during the first several months of start-up, the plant manager remarked that

> [Schipke's] personal faith and public commitment to the success of the project was a terribly important factor. I tried to display the same confidence to my people. In March, with the line still not running consistently to plan as the production rate stepped up again, Roger invited the media in here to view GE's state-of-the-art automation. Then in early April we had a visit by security analysts for consumer products, and late in April Jack Welch visited and gave his stamp of approval. There was a hell of a lot of exposure during this period.

Leadership factors also played an important role in the case history of Allen-Bradley's CIM, discussed in Chapter 6. The manager appointed to head the new unit while the CIM was in the early design stage possessed a unique combination of experience in equipment design, computer applications, and managing skilled workers. The implementation committee he headed was in charge of laying out the facility and coordinating and working on the design of incoming equipment. He immersed himself in his tasks, assembling the new product by hand to learn what was required of the new equipment, and attending closely to the details of managing the motivation and learning of CIM operators as they debugged and started up the equipment.

The role of leadership is too pervasive and often too subtle to be captured by formal propositions. Nevertheless, strong and positive leadership is crucial to effective implementation of IT— to shaping the context, championing the development process, and staying the course during introduction and diffusion.

NOTES

Preface

1. F. Warren McFarlan and James L. McKenney, *Corporate Information Systems Management: The Issues Facing Senior Executives* (Homewood, Ill.: Richard D. Irwin, 1983); Marc S. Gerstein, *The Technology Connection: Strategy and Change in the Information Age* (Reading, Mass.: Addison-Wesley, 1987); Cyrus F. Gibson and Barbara Bund Jackson, *The Information Imperative* (Lexington, Mass.: Lexington Books, 1987); Peter G.W. Keen, *Computing in Time: Using Telecommunications for Competitive Advantage* (Cambridge, Mass.: Ballinger, 1988); Richard J. Long, *New Office Information Technology: Human and Managerial Implications* (New York: Croom Helm, 1987); Shoshana Zuboff, *In the Age of the Smart Machine: The Future of Work and Power* (New York: Basic Books, 1988); and Calvin Pava, *Managing New Office Technology* (New York: Free Press, 1983).

Introduction and Overview

1. Terri L.G. Hughson, "Implementation Direction: Model and Review," Carnegie-Mellon University Graduate School of Industrial Administration, September 1986.
2. Tora K. Bikson, Cathleen Stasz, and Donald A. Mankin, "Computer-Mediated Work: Individual and Organizational Impact in One Corporate Headquarters," Rand, Santa Monica, Calif., November 1985.
3. Jan Gugliotti and Adam Crescenzi, "Solving the Systems Development Dilemma," *Indication* (May–June 1988): 1–7.
4. Paul S. Goodman and Terri L. Griffith, "Implementation of New Technology," Carnegie-Mellon University Graduate School of Industrial Administration, February 1989.

Chapter 1

1. John Krafcik, "High-Performance Manufacturing: An International Study of Auto Assembly Practice," working paper, MIT International Motor Ve-

hicle Research Project, 1988; and Thomas A. Kochan, "On the Human Side of Technology," *ICL Technical Journal* (November 1988): 391–400.

2. Ramchandran Jaikumar, "Post-Industrial Manufacturing," *Harvard Business Review* (November–December 1986): 69–76.

3. Ibid., 70.

4. Richard E. Walton, *Innovating to Compete: Lessons for Diffusing and Managing Change in the Workplace* (San Francisco: Jossey-Bass, 1987).

5. National Research Council, "Human Resource Practices for Implementing Advanced Manufacturing Technologies" (Washington, D.C.: National Academy Press, 1986).

6. Calvin Pava, *Managing New Office Technology* (New York: Free Press, 1983).

7. Paul S. Adler, "Effective Implementation of Integrated CAD/CAM: A Research Agenda," working paper, Stanford University Industrial Engineering, September 1985.

8. Richard E. Walton and Wendy Vittori, "New Information Technology: Organizational Problem or Opportunity," *Office: Technology and People* (1983): 249–73.

9. James I. Cash and Benn R. Konsynski, "IS Redraws Competitive Boundaries," *Harvard Business Review* (March–April 1985): 134–42.

10. James L. McKenney, Victor S. Doherty, and John J. Sviokla, "An Appraisal of How Task Evolution Influences Choice and Use of Communication Media in Management," working paper, Harvard Business School, October 1988.

11. Robert I. Benjamin and Michael S. Scott Morton, "Information Technology and Organizational Change," working paper 86-017, MIT Sloan School of Management, April 1986.

12. Cyrus F. Gibson and Barbara Bund Jackson, *The Information Imperative* (Lexington, Mass.: Lexington Books, 1987).

13. Shoshana Zuboff, "Automate/Informate: The Two Faces of Intelligent Technology," *Organization Dynamics* (Autumn 1985): 4–18.

14. F. Warren McFarlan and James L. McKenney, *Corporate Information Systems Management: The Issues Facing Senior Executives* (Homewood, Ill.: Richard D. Irwin, 1983), 52.

15. Shoshana Zuboff, *In the Age of the Smart Machine: The Future of Work and Power* (New York: Basic Books, 1988).

16. See Michael J. Piori and Charles F. Sable, *The Second Industrial Divide* (New York: Basic Books, 1984); Michael Maccoby, *Why Work: Leading the New Generation* (New York: Simon & Schuster, 1988); and Zuboff, *In the Age of the Smart Machine.*

17. See Richard E. Walton, "Social Choice in the Development of Advanced Information Technology," *Technology in Society* 4 (1982): 41–49; and Zuboff, *In the Age of the Smart Machine.*

18. Joel D. Goldhar and Mariann Jelinek, "Plan for Economies of Scope,"

Harvard Business Review (November–December 1983): 141–48; and Robert H. Hayes and Ramchandran Jaikumar, "Manufacturing's Crisis: New Technologies, Obsolete Organizations," *Harvard Business Review* (September–October 1988): 77–85.

19. John S. Carroll and Constance Perin, "How Expectations About Microcomputers Influence Their Organizational Consequences," working paper 88-044, MIT Sloan School of Management, April 1988.

20. Dorothy Leonard-Barton, "The Case for Integrative Innovation: An Expert System at Digital," *Sloan Management Review* (Fall 1987): 7–19.

21. McFarlan and McKenney, *Corporate Information Systems Management,* 52.

22. Constance Perin, "The Moral Fabric of the Office: Organizational Habits vs. High-Tech Options for Work Schedule Flexibilities," working paper 2011-88, MIT Sloan School of Management, May 1988.

23. Lynda M. Applegate, James I. Cash, Jr., and D. Quinn Mills, "Information Technology and Tomorrow's Manager," *Harvard Business Review* (November–December 1988): 128–36.

24. William J. Bruns, Jr., and F. Warren McFarlan, "Information Puts Power in Control Systems," *Harvard Business Review* (September–October 1987): 89–94.

25. Oscar Hauptman and Thomas J. Allen, "The Influence of Communication Technologies on Organizational Structure: A Conceptual Model for Future Research," working paper 87-038, MIT Sloan School of Management, May 1987.

Chapter 2

1. I draw upon many sources for this account of Mrs. Fields Inc.: My own interview with Randy Fields and a regional manager in February 1989; Tom Richman, "Mrs. Fields' Secret Ingredient," *Inc* (October 1987): 65–72; Keri Ostrofsky and James I. Cash, Jr., "Mrs. Fields Cookies," Harvard Business School Case Services, 9-189-056, Harvard Business School, 1988; and Debbi Fields, *One Smart Cookie* (New York: Simon & Schuster, 1987).

2. See, for example, Buck Brown, "How the Cookie Crumbled at Mrs. Fields," *The Wall Street Journal* (June 2, 1988): B1. This article speculates that the company was too late in diversifying its store menu, wrong in taking the concept to Europe, and overextended itself when it acquired La Petite Boulangerie.

3. Richman, "Mrs. Fields' Secret Ingredient," 66.

4. Ibid., 67.

5. Ibid., 66.

6. Ibid., 67.

7. Ostrofsky and Cash, "Mrs. Fields Cookies," 3.

8. Richman, "Mrs. Fields' Secret Ingredient," 66.

9. Randy Fields interview.
10. Richman, "Mrs. Fields' Secret Ingredient," 72.

Chapter 3

1. Archie McGill, "Some Thoughts on Creative Organizational Change," *Stage by Stage* (September–October 1986): 16–17.
2. See Jack Rockart, "The Line Takes the Leadership," working paper 87-039, MIT Sloan School of Management, August 1987; F. Warren McFarlan and James L. McKenney, *Corporate Information Systems Management: The Issues Facing Senior Executives* (Homewood, Ill.: Richard D. Irwin, 1983); and Richard L. Nolan and Alex J. Pollack, "Organization and Architecture, or Architecture and Organization," *Stage by Stage* (September–October 1986): 1–10.
3. Alfred D. Chandler, Jr., *Strategy and Structure: Chapters in the History of the Industrial Enterprise* (Cambridge, Mass.: MIT Press, 1962).
4. Raymond E. Miles and Charles C. Snow, *Organization Strategy, Structure, and Process* (New York: McGraw-Hill, 1978).
5. Rosabeth Moss Kanter, *Change Masters* (New York: Simon & Schuster, 1983).
6. See D. Tapscott, *Office Automation: A User-Driven Method* (New York: Plenum Press, 1982); G.L. Parsons, "Information Technology: A New Competitive Weapon," *Sloan Management Review* 25 (Fall 1983): 3–14; and Gerald I. Susman and James W. Dean, Jr., "Strategic Use of Computer-Integrated Manufacturing in the Emerging Competitive Environment," Pennsylvania State University Center for the Management of Technological and Organizational Change, October 1988.
7. See Jack F. Rockart and Michael S. Scott Morton, "Implications of Changes in Information Technology for Corporate Strategy," *Interfaces* (January–February 1984): 84–95; Michael E. Porter and Victor E. Millar, "How Information Gives You Competitive Advantage," *Harvard Business Review* (July–August 1985): 149–60; and F. Warren McFarlan, "Information Technology Changes the Way You Compete," *Harvard Business Review* (May–June 1984): 98–103.
8. McFarlan and McKenney, *Corporate Information Systems Management,* 83–84.
9. I draw upon two pieces of material reporting on this case: James W. Dean, Jr., *Deciding to Innovate: How Firms Justify Advanced Technology* (Cambridge, Mass.: Ballinger, 1987), 41–58; and James W. Dean, Jr., "Building the Future: The Justification Process for Advanced Manufacturing Technology," working paper 86-9, Pennsylvania State University Center for Management of Technology and Organizational Change, June 1986.
10. Dean, *Deciding to Innovate,* 50.
11. Ibid., 52.

12. Ibid.
13. Beth Ann Lewis, "Eastman Kodak's Implementation of Micro-Based Manufacturing Software in Decentralized Organizations: A Human Resource Perspective," master's thesis, MIT Sloan School of Management, May 1988.
14. Edgar H. Schein and Diane D. Wilson, "How Top Executives Feel About Computers," *New York Times* (August 21, 1988): F4.
15. Rockart, "The Line Takes the Leadership."
16. Richard E. Walton and Wendy Vittori, "New Information Technology: Organizational Problem or Opportunity," *Office: Technology and People* (1983): 249–73.

Chapter 4

1. National Research Council, "Human Resource Practices for Implementing Advanced Manufacturing Technology" (Washington, D.C.: National Academy Press, 1986): 2.
2. Ibid., 5.
3. Richard Morano and Jeanne Leonardi, "Xerox's Critical Skills Training Program: A Commitment to Retraining Pays Off," in Jill Casner-Lotto and Associates (eds.), *Successful Training Strategies* (San Francisco: Jossey-Bass, 1988), 345–58.
4. Ibid., 348–49.
5. John V. Hickey, "The Travelers Corporation: Expanding Computer Literacy in the Organization," in Jill Casner-Lotto and Associates (eds.), *Successful Training Strategies* (San Francisco: Jossey-Bass, 1988), 19–34.
6. John Chalykoff, "Determinants of Employees' Affective Response to the Use of Information Technology in Monitoring Performance," working paper 88-042, MIT Sloan School of Management, January 1988.
7. William Lazonick, "Value Creation on the Shop Floor: Skill, Effort, and Technology in U.S. and Japanese Manufacturing," working paper, Harvard Business School, February 1988.
8. Richard E. Walton, "Challenges in the Management of Technology and Labor Relations," in Richard E. Walton and Paul Lawrence (eds.), *HRM: Trends and Challenges* (Boston: Harvard Business School Press, 1985), 199–216; and Richard E. Walton and Robert B. McKersie, "Managing New Technology and Labor Relations: An Opportunity for Mutual Influence," paper presented at conference sponsored by the Panel on Technology and Employment of the National Academy of Sciences and the Department of Labor, October 1988.
9. Rosabeth Moss Kanter, "The New Alliances: How Strategic Partnerships Are Reshaping American Business," in Herbert L. Sawyer (ed.), *Business in the Contemporary World* (Lanham, Md.: University Press of America, 1988), 59–82.

10. National Research Council, "Human Resource Practices," 4.
11. D. Quinn Mills, *The IBM Lesson* (New York: Time Books, 1988).
12. Jerome M. Rosow and Robert Zager, "Training for New Technology, Part II: Toward Continuous Learning," report of the Work in America Institute, Inc., Scarsdale, N.Y., 1986.
13. Ibid., 7.

Chapter 5

1. James W. Dean, Jr., *Deciding to Innovate: How Firms Justify Advanced Technology* (Cambridge, Mass.: Ballinger, 1987), 136.
2. Rick Herbert, memo dated June 8, 1987.
3. Gloria Schuck and Shoshana Zuboff, "Data Administration in Citibank Brazil (A): The Competitive Advantage," Harvard Business School Case Services, 9-486-109, Harvard Business School, 1986.
4. Shoshana Zuboff, *In the Age of the Smart Machine: The Future of Work and Power* (New York: Basic Books, 1988).
5. Schuck and Zuboff, "Data Administration."
6. Ibid.
7. Ibid.
8. Ibid.
9. Ibid.
10. Robert J. Thomas, "Organizational Politics and Technological Change," working paper 2035-88, MIT Sloan School of Management, July 1988; idem, "Technological Choice: Obstacles and Opportunities for Union-Management Consultation on New Technology," working paper 1987-88, MIT Sloan School of Management, January 1989 (rev.).
11. Herbert, memo dated June 8, 1987.

Chapter 6

1. Joel Fadem, "National Background, Automation, and Work Design in the United States," in F. Butera and J.E. Thurman (eds.), *Automation and Work Design* (New York: North-Holland, 1984), 691.
2. Lotte Bailyn, "Freeing Work from the Constraints of Location and Time: An Analysis Based on Data from the United Kingdom," working paper 87-037, MIT Sloan School of Management, April 1986.
3. See R.E. Rice and E.M. Rogers, "Reinvention in the Innovation Process," *Knowledge,* no. 4 (1980): 499–514; and Dorothy Leonard-Barton, "Implementation as Mutual Adaptation of Technology and Organization," *Research Policy* 17 (1988): 251–67.
4. Richard E. Walton, "New Technology and Job Design in a Phone Company (A) and (B)," Harvard Business School Case Services, 9-483-073 and 9-483-074, Harvard Business School, 1982.

5. J. R. Hackman, R. Janson Oldham, and K. Purdy, "A New Strategy for Job Enrichment," *California Management Review* (Summer 1975): 62.

6. Fadem, "National Background," 689–690.

7. Ibid., 690.

8. Louis Davis and Charles Sullivan, "A Labour-management Contract and Quality of Working Life," *Journal of Occupational Behavior* 1, no. 1 (1980): 29–41.

9. Sabra Goldstein and Janice Klein, "Allen-Bradley (A) and (B)," Harvard Business School Case Services, 9-687-073 and 9-687-074, Harvard Business School, 1987.

10. Goldstein and Klein, "Allen-Bradley (B)."

11. National Research Council, "Human Resource Practices for Implementing Advanced Manufacturing Technology" (Washington, D.C.: National Academy Press, 1986).

12. Richard E. Walton and Gerald I. Susman, "People Policies for the New Machines," *Harvard Business Review* (March–April 1987): 98–106.

13. Hackman et al., "A New Strategy for Job Enrichment," 62.

14. Calvin Pava, *Managing New Office Technology* (New York: Free Press, 1983).

15. Constance Perin, "The Moral Fabric of the Office: Organizational Habits vs. High-Tech Options for Work Schedule Flexibilities," working paper 2011-88, MIT Sloan School of Management, May 1988.

16. Shoshana Zuboff, *In the Age of the Smart Machine: The Future of Work and Power* (New York: Basic Books, 1988).

Chapter 7

1. Gloria Bronsema and Shoshana Zuboff, "The Expense Tracking System at Tiger Creek," Harvard Business School Case Services, 9-485-057, Harvard Business School, 1984.

2. Enid Mumford, "Participative Systems Design: Structure and Method," *Systems, Objectives, Solutions* 1, no. 1 (1981): 5–19.

3. Bronsema and Zuboff, "The Expense Tracking System."

4. Shoshana Zuboff, *In the Age of the Smart Machine: The Future of Work and Power* (New York: Basic Books, 1988).

5. Bronsema and Zuboff, "The Expense Tracking System."

6. Ibid.

7. Ibid.

8. Ibid.

9. Ibid.

10. Ibid.

11. Dorothy Leonard-Barton, "The Case for Integrative Innovation: An Expert System at Digital," *Sloan Management Review* (Fall 1987): 7–19.

12. Ibid.

13. Ibid., 11.
14. John Henderson, "Cooperative Behavior in Information Systems Planning and Design," working paper 88-041, MIT Sloan School of Management, January 1988.

Chapter 8

1. Kendal and Nationwide Video Rentals are disguised names.
2. The assessment team included Gloria Schuck, Shoshana Zuboff, and myself. The diagnosis presented here draws upon the collaborative assessment but is attributable solely to the author.
3. Ramchandran Jaikumar, "Flexible Manufacturing Systems: A Managerial Perspective," draft working paper, Harvard Business School, January 1984.
4. Shoshana Zuboff, *In the Age of the Smart Machine: The Future of Work and Power* (New York: Basic Books, 1988).

Chapter 9

1. Brian T. Pentland, "AES at IRS: An Interactionist View of the Automation of Professional Work," second-year paper, MIT Sloan School of Management, January 1988.
2. Dorothy Leonard-Barton, "The Case for Integrative Innovation: An Expert Systems at Digitial," *Sloan Management Review* (Fall 1987): 7.
3. Ibid., 13.
4. John S. Carroll and Constance Perin, "How Expectations About Microcomputers Influence Their Organizational Consequences," working paper 88-044, MIT Sloan School of Management, April 1988.
5. Pentland, "AES at IRS"; idem., "Implementation of Enduser Computing in the Internal Revenue Service," working paper, MIT Sloan School of Management, January 1989.
6. Pentland, "AES at IRS."
7. Pentland, "Implementation of Enduser Computing."

INDEX

A

B

C